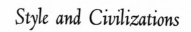

Style and Civilizations

## BY A. L. KROEBER

# Style and Civilizations

GREENWOOD PRESS, PUBLISHERS
WESTPORT, CONNECTICUT

Library of Congress Cataloging in Publication Data

Kroeber, Alfred Louis, 1876-1960.
   Style and civilizations.

   Reprint of the ed. published by Cornell University
Press, Ithaca, New York.
   1.  Civilization--Philosophy.  I.  Title.
[CB19.K687  1973]           901.9          73-8560
ISBN  0-8371-6966-6

First published in 1957 by Cornell University Press,
Ithaca, New York

Reissued in 1973 by Greenwood Press by arrangement
with the original publisher, Cornell University Press

Reprinted in 1973 by Greenwood Press, Inc.,
51 Riverside Avenue, Westport, Conn. 06880

Library of Congress catalog card number 73-8560
ISBN 0-8371-6966-6

Printed in the United States of America

10 9 8 7 6 5 4 3 2

# Contents

*Style and Civilizations*

# 1

# Kinds and Properties
## of Styles

MY ULTIMATE aim in these chapters is an inquiry into civilization: what are its characteristics, its essential nature, its features in the past, its future prospects. We know that civilizations happen: they have a course, they are achieved. We know something of these courses and their achievements; but we understand very little of what makes them. Civilizations obviously are among the most complex groups of phenomena of which we have cognizance. Perhaps they are even more subtle than complex. Phenomena of great intricacy presumably are due to intricate causes. Experience has shown that it is hopeless to storm, by a frontal attack, the great citadels of the causality underlying highly complex groups of facts. They yield slowly before methods of science or scholarship developed step by step, systematically, cumulatively. We possess only partial and scattered techniques as yet to help us answer why civilizations are as they are. I therefore renounce at the outset any claim of presenting new enlightenment on what originates and shapes civilizations. Before such understanding of cause can be validly attained, we must better understand the effects; namely, the qualities and traits of civilizations. The what and the how must be determined, analyzed, and organized before we can hope to penetrate adequately to their why.

I hope to review some of the more notable thinking of the past century on the nature of civilizations. Particularly do I wish to try to stress an aspect which most writers on the subject have understressed, and some have been almost unaware of: namely, the factor of style.

Style as a generic concept is broad but remains ill defined. It needs exploration as to its general properties. On the other hand, particular styles are often seen to be highly definite in their qualities. They are distinctive, and they are readily recognized by those interested. They can even have strong predictive value. An object of unknown source or origin, well made in a defined style, can be historically assigned to that style with assurance. Often such an object can be assigned a date, a specific position in the course of development of its style. In this way, art objects become sensitive and reliable evidence as to historic connections previously unknown or unsuspected. Whoever has studied art history, or has worked in the archaeology of even the simpler cultures, will attest this.

Let us begin with dictionary definitions of style; or rather with a conspectus of the welter of definitions which, in the interest of total inclusiveness, a large dictionary presents for a word of such imprecise boundary of meaning as style. Three main lines of reference emerge. Style is characteristic; it is distinctive; it refers to manner or mode.

The etymology is from *stylus*, the pointed rod used for writing on wax by Greeks and Romans. The sense here is metaphorical, as we speak of an inspiring or a poisoned pen, of a fluent or a bold hand. A man's style originally was his characteristic, idiosyncratic manner of writing: possibly at first with emphasis on the shapes of his letters, his handwriting, certainly later with reference rather to his choice and combination of words. It was always an individual's style in the beginning—a sense which the word still includes, though it has acquired also a social sense.

Just so, by further metaphorical extension, the denotation of the word style has spread from literature to all the arts: for instance, the Gothic style of architecture, the contrapuntal style of music. We speak legitimately of the individual style of Monet within the style of the impressionist movement in late nineteenth-century painting. In fact, in modern art history and aesthetic criticism the word style perhaps more often carries its social than its individual denotation. My reference, in this book, will of course be generally to the social aspect, since civilization is a sociocultural phenomenon.

In nonaesthetical, everyday low-brow usage, style probably refers first of all to dress, next to bodily surroundings and appurtenances: "It won't be a stylish marriage, I can't afford a carriage."

Of late decades the form "stylized" has had considerable vogue. It usually denotes an accentuation of certain abstractable forms as over against the content or subject matter: a formally emphasized, distinctive manner of representing things.

When a motor car is "styled," an aesthetically significant form or surface is added to its functional structure and purposes. The "styling" of the text of a book by a publisher is something very different from the literary style in which the author has written it. It deals with regularity of capitalization, punctuation, spelling, and other tactical matters of typographical orderliness, and from there proceeds back a certain way toward visual aesthetic standards of headings, spacing, and make-up of the physical volume. Clearly, the meanings of style have become many.

However, all the more central usages of the word refer first to form as against substance, manner as against content. Second, they imply some consistency of forms. And third, they may suggest that the forms used in the style cohere sufficiently to integrate into a series of related patterns.

While style refers primarily to aesthetic qualities, and while it constitutes perhaps the essence of the fine arts, it can certainly be traced also in those activities which result in useful or practical arts as well as in the pleasure-giving or aesthetic ones. Gastronomy is an example. Here we have, first of all, basic and long-term styles of food preparation characteristic of vast areas, and sometimes typically associated with great civilizations. In East Asia, for instance, food is prepared soft: boiled rice, or wheat in paste rather than in bread; meat and vegetable cut into bits in the kitchen, not at the table or by the eater—hence a tendency to combine several foods into one prepared dish. The origin of this specialized manner of cooking is obscure. It may possibly have been due to, or suggested in the first place by, certain properties of available materials, such as rice being naturally more palatable to human beings husked, unground, and boiled, whereas wheat is more satisfactory ground into meal and baked. However that may be, the significance is less in the start than in the consequences, namely, the habits applied to almost all foods, their preparation, service, accompaniments, and utensils. Thus East Asiatic bowls replace our plates, chopsticks our knives and forks; and these in turn entail distinctive postures, manipulations, and etiquettes; which again interadapt with lack of furniture familiar to us, especially chairs. Such differentiations can be more than trivial. For instance, when one learns that Viet Nam eats with chopsticks but Siam and Burma without, it is an immediate conjecture that the former country lies in the orbit of influence of Chinese civilization, the two latter of Indian; which the totality of the cultures confirms. And indeed, Viet Nam's form of Buddhism, its writing, law, administration, theater, and education are Chinese-derived; those of Siam and Burma stem directly from India.

The Indian subcontinent ate, and largely eats, directly from its fingers; so once did most of the millions living from there west to Spain. This habit accords easily with bread being the staple food. In Northern Europe, meat loomed proportionally larger in diet than in the long densely populated, more arid, pasture-poor Mediterranean lands; and the mediaeval custom took hold in the North of each guest bringing his knife to table. Individual forks came in much later, as a luxury imported from the Mediterranean; but they fitted in with heavy meat consumption.

Within these greater areas of civilization, well-marked national styles of cuisine arose: French, Italian, British, Spanish, for instance; or Japanese and Chinese in the Far East. Reference is to more than a favorite national dish: it is to consistent nuances of proportion, seasoning, flavor, resulting in a consistent over-all quality. There are even composite styles, like standard contemporary American cooking, which, starting with a modified English base, has added strains of French and subsequently Italian style, and developed native innovations, such as heavy sweetening, efflorescence of fantastic salads, emphasis on chill, and partial displacement of palatal appeal by eye allure. This last quality, interestingly enough, reappears in Japanese dressing of food as compared with Chinese.

These may be trivialities of mode of life, but they are also qualitative realities of living.

I turn next to styles of dress, which we often speak of as fashions. If I dwell in some detail on these, instead of hastening at once on to fine-art styles, it is not because I consider them intrinsically more interesting, but because dress styles lend themselves more readily to accurate analysis than do styles in the high arts. The generalizations that can be made about fashions can be stated more precisely, and can be supported by more objective evidence. My goal is discussion of style in the fine arts; but the best foundation I can lay for that is in certain conclusions derivable from dress fashions.

There are several considerations involved in women's dress styles. Underlying is the element of utility of clothing, of protection or convenience, which sets a rough frame within which style operates. Next there is the element of erotic allure, often partly sublimated into a seeking for generic aesthetic beauty, though never wholly so. These can both be warped by considerations of social effect, the sumptuary expression of rank, power, wealth, lavishness, waste. And the final determinant of all the preceding is, in all recent civilization, the factor of novelty, of the importance of the moment. In the last analysis this factor of the moment is more influential than generic aesthetic value, over which timeliness has precedence and which it ruthlessly violates. This is evidently a distinctive feature of dress fashions in our civilization:

7

they must never cease changing, even if it be from better to worse. There have been fashion changes also in China and Japan, and in ancient Greece and Rome, but they were less rapid. Their moments lasted longer.

Some measure of change is implied in every style that possesses a degree of creativity. But such change is a function, almost a by-product, of the creative drive; and it can greatly vary in rate. In our dress styles, however, it is the rate of change which tends to be constant, and the drive that creates aesthetic values has to accommodate its operation to this. There is a certain frivolity in this incessant movement for its own sake, which fails to progress from one specific value to another, and which knows neither longer goal nor prepared build-up nor development. It is something like an eternally spinning, slightly undulating top. The degree to which these properties hold true, is what makes dress fashions a unique phenomenon in our society and civilization.

On the other hand, the fact also renders dress fashions rather readily susceptible to analysis by measurement. The particular moment adhered to is always known—all fashion is dated. Then, the elemental contours of fashions, as expressed in the principal proportions or diameters of the outline or silhouette of the dressed person are readily measured on photographs, fashion-plates, or even paintings. In our civilization women's clothing lends itself particularly well to analytic study of this kind because while both the aesthetic and erotic drives are given expression, the rate and extent of change for its own sake are high.

It requires no pedantic study to prove that fashion is in a constant state of seemingly aimless vibrancy and shift: that is the essential property of fashion. But in addition it readily becomes apparent from comparative measurements that there are also long-term drifts which tend to be overlooked and forgotten because fashion designing and dressing are so occupied with being timed to the fleeting moment. These long-term drifts are expressed in fundamental diameters of dress as a whole, such as width and length of skirts and proportion or place of the waist, not in cuffs, frills, flounces, paniers, and other superstructural parts. These last ordinarily live only a few years at a time. The basic proportions, on the other hand, though they too undergo surface fluctuations of a year or two or several, nevertheless show gradual trends, in one direction, of around half a century. It is the features of proportional diameters, which cannot disappear because they are built in, that show the long trends. That is, they cannot disappear short of a fundamental overturn of the style itself—such as pants or drapes displacing skirts. As long as there are skirts, they must have a length and a width. Moreover, when a maximum of physical possibility or manageability has been reached, the style does not hover there long but reverses its course and crawls, for a more or less equal duration, back toward a minimum.

There is thus a slow pendulum-like swing between extremes, in the dress proportions examined, at a fairly even rate of about a century for the full two-way oscillation. This long swing tends to be obscured on a short-range view such as designers and wearers of dresses are bound to take, because of their incessant trying—like the stock market—to focus on the present instant. If they did not, they would promptly be out of fashion—as the stock broker might be bankrupt.

That the long range trends should be oscillatory between possible extremes of wearability seems to most people somehow natural or expectable, once they accept the trends as proven. I agree with them; even though I did not for long see what there was in the phenomena that compelled a trend toward fuller skirts, once it got established, to go progressively on to the wearable limit of fullness, instead of moving perhaps halfway and then reversing. I suspect now that it is because while dress fashion is distinguished, or even dominated, by the principle of incessant change, it also contains a considerable element of purely aesthetic style, and that art styles, while their founders of course cannot foresee the ultimate achievements of the style, nevertheless do usually unfold in a progressive manner until the potentialities contained in the beginning efforts have been exhausted, thus reaching a culmination or "maximum."

This point may be clearer after we have considered fine-art styles more fully. I make it now because it seems of some importance to realize that while dress fashion styles are in their frivolity a sort of minor perversion of fine art styles, they also do contain some properties of the stylistic manifestations of genuine aesthetic creativity.

While we were measuring and tabulating fashion

plates, my colleague Jane Richardson and I could not help but note that dress modes were relatively steady and tranquil during a period which began about 1835 and ended around 1905. Previous to this 70-year calm cycle, there was a period of at least 45 agitated and fluctuating years back to the beginning of our measurable record in 1788. There was also another period of instability and change for the 30 or more years from 1905 to 1936 when we concluded our measurements. This last period may have continued on beyond the span of our data—as the earlier one may have begun before our data commenced in 1788.

It is obvious that the first of the two periods of fashion agitation is pretty much that of the French Revolution, Napoleonic Wars, and post-Napoleonic tensions through the revolutionary attempts of 1830. Equally, the second era of fashion agitation was the period of pre-1914 mounting political tension, of World War I, and of the uneasy inter–World War years. But 1835–1905 coincides almost exactly with the reign of Victoria in England, with peace on the Continent of Europe broken only by brief wars and rapid recuperations—in short the golden nineteenth-century culmination of the industrial, laissez faire, and bourgeois democratic phase of our civilization. The American Civil War had no effect, because high fashions were originating in Europe.

This contrast between relatively placid periods of fashion change and relatively vehement ones is probably of greater significance than the fact of long-time swings between extremes, because of its seeming connection or correlation with periods of much larger events of history. Why should decades of social and political unrest affect women's clothes at all? Why should for instance skirts be narrow but waists wide in an agitated time, and then reverse as peaceful contentment settles on the civilized world? Why these particular results? And through what mechanism?

Instead of guessing at the cause, the first need seemed to be to confirm the impression that there really was a correlation. And this meant going back to our original measurements and extracting from them the year-by-year variability of dress fashions. How much did the individual dresses produced in one year differ from each other as compared with another year? This variability is most simply expressed by noting each deviation from the average, and then calculating the standard deviation, the orthodox basic measure of variability. A higher deviation denotes greater variability. When several different dimensions are compared, these standard deviations are converted into percentages—technically, coefficients of variability, or symbol: "V."

Since lists of figures can be difficult to follow, I have converted the variabilities into black and white symbols for five-year averages. If the variability for a quinquennium was low, there is a white or blank space in the diagram. If it was high, there is a cross. If it was very high— two times or three times as great as the median variability —there are two or three crosses.

For instance, in the first column of Table 1, which stands for skirt length, the first space contains a cross, but

# Graphic Table 1

Intensity of Variability in Women's Dress-Fashion Styles as Shown by Five-Year Means of Fluctuation Units Representing Approximate Medians of Percentaged Standard Deviations within Each Year. (Each cross denotes one fluctuation unit of size stated.)

| Fluctuation Unit | Skirt Length | Skirt Width | Waist Length | Waist Width | Decolletage Depth | Decolletage Width |
|---|---|---|---|---|---|---|
| | 1.6 | 17 | 7 | 9 | 13 | 14.5 |
| 1787–91 | X | | X | X | XX | X |
| 1792–96 | | | | | XX | X |
| 1797–1801 | | | X | X | X | |
| 1802–06 | | X | X | | X | |
| 1807–11 | X | XX | X | X | X | X |
| 1812–16 | XX | X | X | | X | X |
| 1817–21 | X | | X | | | |
| 1822–26 | X | | X | | | |
| 1827–31 | X | | X | X | | |
| 1832–36 | X | | | | | X |
| 1837–41 | | | | X | X | X |
| 1842–46 | | | | | | |
| 1847–51 | | | | | | |
| 1852–56 | | | | | | |
| 1857–61 | | | | X | | |
| 1862–66 | | | | | | |
| 1867–71 | | | | | | |
| 1872–76 | | | | | | X |
| 1877–81 | | X | | | | |
| 1882–86 | X | X | | X | | |
| 1887–91 | | X | | X | | |
| 1892–96 | | X | X | X | | X |
| 1897–1901 | | | | X | X | X |
| 1902–06 | | | | | X | X |
| 1907–11 | | X | | X | X | X |
| 1912–16 | XX | XX | X | X | X | |
| 1917–21 | XX | XX | X | X | X | X |
| 1922–26 | XX | XX | XX | X | X | X |
| 1927–31 | XX | X | X | XX | X | X |
| 1932–36 | X | X | X | XX | XX | XX |

the next three are blank, which means that variability averaged fairly low in that feature for the twenty years 1787–1806, the years including the French Revolution —which took place, by the way, in the Paris which was then, as it is now, the center of fashion origination for women's *haute couture*. But the fifth and sixth spaces, for 1807–1816, covering most of Napoleon's empire, show a cross and then two crosses, which means that skirt length variability averaged double-high. The next four spaces are again marked, though not with a double cross: that is, they are high. But with them, around 1836, we have reached the boundary of the first era of dress style agitation, and we now enter the long Victorian calm of fashion—seven long decades of tranquillity: this middle part of our column is blankly white with only one exception.

Then, with 1912—still going on down the first column—black unsettlement raises its head once more, and with double crosses: we are entering the period of World War I and ensuing unrest.

I should have liked to resume the investigation and carry the record on over the twenty years that would bring us down to 1956 and today. But to assemble the necessary plates or photographs, to select those that adequately show all the six dimensions, to measure these, to convert the gross figures to percentages, to average these and compute their standard deviations, then to check each of these operations—all this is a matter of months of application.

The second column, that for width of skirt, is generally similar to the first, but differs in some details. In this second column, the climax of the first era of unsettlement begins and ends a little earlier. Also, there are two decades of agitation—though not of very high agitation —before the end of the Victorian calm. Similarly throughout: no two columns show exactly the same distribution of the crosses of instability. But none of the six columns even begins to violate the generic pattern common to the rest. This pattern is obvious: an early era of 40 to 50 years of prevailingly high variability—33 times high as against 27 low, or 24 against 12 up to 1816; then 70 years of low variability, with three-fourths or more of the spaces "calm"; and then another 30 years with every quinquennium in every dimension appearing as mainly fluctuating, agitated, and marked—sometimes with double crosses. These 30 analyzed years out of the past 50 manifest high variability even more consistently than the 70 Victorian years manifested low variability. The dress style from 1907 to 1936 clearly suggests persistent unsettlement and strain. I am genuinely sorry to have nothing on the past 20 years. If I were to guess, it would be that variability has moderated: that we are by now over the hump of restlessness. But guesses are free, and cheap; so let us return to findings supported by evidence.

Of the six dimensions, the one that best reflects the general pattern of how women's dress styles behaved during the 150 years dealt with would clearly be "Waist Length," or waist position, in the third column. It is almost solidly marked until 1836, almost solidly blank until 1906, almost solidly marked from then on. In a moment, I hope to be able to show why it is this measure that best expresses the general trend of fashion in our 150 years.

There is another measure of instability of dress style which we used that I do not want to linger on, but do want to show the results for corroboration. This method compares the simple average for a year with a moving average for five years. The difference between the straight and the moving average is in itself a difference between fluctuating irregularity and more stable regularity—or more precisely, continuous change. By expressing this difference in terms of "fluctuation units" to equalize conditions for the six dimensions, we get a second measure of variability which is graphed herewith in Table 2.

Again the crosses are abundant at the top, but in the 1827–1836 decade they begin to die away, and then there is a long white period when there are almost none. Around the turn of the century, the crosses hesitatingly begin to reappear—much like sunspots on renewal of their cycle, except that the fashion-style cycle is much longer than the 11-year astronomical solar one. With the outbreak of World War I the crosses come thicker and remain in full frequency as far as the record continues.

The clue that leads toward interpretation is this. What we have just established is that there exist fairly long periods of high fashion variability alternating with periods of low variability. Since in general these periods of high variability coincide pretty closely with periods of high sociopolitical tension and insecurity, it is tempting to correlate the two as respectively effect and cause. I do

Intensity of Variability in Women's Dress-Fashion Styles as Shown by Five-Year Means of Frequency of Fluctuation Units Representing Degree of Deviation of Mean-for-Year from Five-Year Moving-Average. (Each cross denotes one fluctuation unit of size stated.)

| | Skirt | | Waist | | Decolletage | |
| | Length | Width | Length | Width | Depth | Width |
| Fluctuation Unit | 1.5 | 7 | 4 | 6 | 7 | 9 |
|---|---|---|---|---|---|---|
| 1788–91 | | | x | xxx | xx | x |
| 1792–96 | | x | x | xx | xx | x |
| 1797–1801 | | | | xx | x | |
| 1802–06 | x | x | | | x | x |
| 1807–11 | | x | x | | | |
| 1812–16 | x | x | x | | x | |
| 1817–21 | x | | xx | x | xx | x |
| 1822–26 | x | | x | x | x | x |
| 1827–31 | | | x | x | | |
| 1832–36 | x | | | | | x |
| 1837–41 | | | | | | |
| 1842–46 | | | | | | |
| 1847–51 | | | | | | |
| 1852–56 | | | | | | |
| 1857–61 | | | | | | |
| 1862–66 | | | | | | |
| 1867–71 | | | | | | |
| 1872–76 | | | | | | |
| 1877–81 | | | | | | |
| 1882–86 | | | | | | |
| 1887–91 | | | | | | |
| 1892–96 | | | | | | |
| 1897–1901 | | x | | | | x |
| 1902–06 | | | | | x | x |
| 1907–11 | | x | | | | |
| 1912–16 | x | x | | | | x |
| 1917–21 | x | xxx | | | | |
| 1922–26 | xx | x | x | | | |
| 1927–31 | xxx | x | x | x | x | |
| 1932–34 | | | | xx | x | x |

not, however, believe that this frontal attempt to explain style changes directly from social-psychological conditions is fruitful. Even if fashion variability indicates unsettlement and insecurity, and unsettling sociopolitical events tend to bring about widespread generic insecurity, and it therefore seems plausible to connect the two causally, the correlation remains selective, and therefore incomplete as an explanation, and perhaps arbitrary. The Napoleonic era is also one of climax of minimum width and minimum length of skirts, and of maximum thickness of waist in fashion. Can we hold the Emperor and his continental convulsions responsible for producing an extreme of shortened dresses and widened waists? The question itself suggests a certain ridiculousness of disproportion: a vast mountain of cause bringing forth a highly specific mousetail of fashion effect.

If we take refuge in the fact that a century later the World War period was also accompanied by short and narrow skirts and wide waists, we have here indeed a second case of correlation, and therefore a bit of encouragement that we may be on the track of some little natural law of style change. But the disproportion between vast generic cause and minutely specific effect is still with us.

In addition, there is one proportion in which fashion moved in opposite direction in the two periods of stress. This is length or position of the waist. Around 1800, the waistline moved up to its minimum, right under the breasts. After 1900, it moved downward to its all-time maximum, at the hips. Evidently then, there is no specific and rigorous "law" involved, that great wars and their accompaniments regularly bring on certain particular extremes of women's dress proportions; which indeed would be contrary to common-sense expectability.

This particular contrary-moving fashion trait also gives a clue on how the actual connection between wars and fashion is to be traced. We need not doubt the generic finding that the unsettlement of the times is communicated to fashions—that they are influenced and also become unsettled. But the *how* of the unsettlement of dress style is *not* dictated by the sociopolitical conditions; that must be due to something in the set of the fashions themselves—something within the structure of fashion, so to speak, at the time when the unsettling larger influences impinge on them.

This intervening structural factor which is needed to convert our causality from a fantastic to a probable explanation is what I call the "basic pattern" of modern Western women's dress style. It is a conceptual construct, empirically derived from the phenomena of the history of Western fashion. It is also an ideal implicit in the style itself, a half-conscious value sought for by the style. And intellectually, it serves as a "model" by which to explain and better understand a complex series of happenings.

As characteristic of this underlying pattern or model which serves as an equilibrium in Western women's dress styles, I assume or posit an ideal silhouette dominated by a skirt that spreads amply full and reaches to the feet, falling from a waist that is as slender as possible and is in normal, anatomical position. Below the waistline, or at any rate below the hips, the Western ideal skirt departs drastically and deliberately from anatomy: it provides a substitute for the legs of nature. Above the hips, however, the dress contour follows the contours of the body, including upper breast, shoulders, and arms when protection is convenient or necessary, but tending to leave these expanses uncovered in situations of formality or display.

This basic ideal pattern of Western women's dress, mediaeval and modern, has gone through a thousand years of constant remodeling without any fundamental change. It differs markedly from the basic pattern of ancient Mediterranean dress—Egyptian, Greek, Roman—in which there was no skirt as such, in which both waist and legs were neither emphasized nor de-emphasized, but accent was on long line and folds of drapery down the entire body. No part of the anatomical figure was specially concealed, no part was specially revealed or exaggerated in the ancient Mediterranean pattern.

A third basic or ideal pattern, also firmly rooted and long enduring, is that of the Far East. Here, perhaps in conformity with racial Mongolian anatomy, much as the Western pattern conformed to characteristic Caucasian female body build, there was no modulation of bosom, waist, and pelvis, but rather was their differentiation obliterated by straight-hanging long jackets or butterfly-bowed loose sashes at the waist; and the Western skirt was replaced by long sleeved coats or draped garments hung from the shoulders; or, in later China, by trousers. There is also an old tendency in the Far East to favor breadth of figure even to the point of squatness—perhaps because it was the superior person that was shown seated, and because elevation on chairs reached China late and Japan even later. The Mediterranean pattern, contrariwise, sought the erect, elongated posture; and while the European skirt aimed at artificial breadth, the upper part of the dress did not.

In these basic patterns of dress fashion we evidently have a phenomenon analogous to the basic styles of cuisine and gastronomy with their ramifications. They are expressions of something long enduring in the civilization.

It is also clear that the basic or ideal pattern of dress links fashion with basic styles in the fine arts. The difference is that fine arts spend much of their course evolving their ideal or goal, where dress fashions seem rather, unconsciously, to take this goal for granted, and then spend most their conscious attention and effort ceaselessly modifying it, Tantalus-like, under the tyrannical spur of mode.

With this basic, ideal, or model pattern in mind, we can now return to our wars and revolutions as influences. All that these sociopolitical tensions seem really to do, is to impart generic tension, upset, and instability to designers of fashion and to the audience and clientele that designers and purveyors serve. When this happens, fashion style then works *against* its basic pattern, as this has been expressed in preceding periods of calm and stability when attention of the mode was directed to minor and superstructural changes—to frills and flounces rather than to fundamental contour. With tension, the basic pattern itself is attacked, violated, inverted. The normally wide and long skirt becomes narrow and short, the normally slender waist is thickened, its position is dislocated.

Now the full and long skirt, the slender waist, are themselves extremes or near-extremes of silhouette, even though they be "normal" as part of the satisfied basic pattern; so that when this pattern is disturbed or assaulted, movement can occur only in one direction: toward the opposite extreme. On the contrary, the naturally "normal" or ideal position of the waist is a midway thing. When this feature comes under pressure, it can move two ways: up or down. This is what happened. In the decade after 1800, the waistline moved up against the bosom. But in the quarter century after 1900, it moved down on to the hips. The precise factors that caused one shift to be up and the other down remain to be discovered. But both shifts are, equally, violations of underlying pattern. It is also evident that both shifts, upward and downward, were necessarily accompanied about equally by an unnatural thickening of the waist diameter, which in turn exaggerated their own effect.

What we have then is, first, a relation between sociopolitical condition of tension and a corresponding tension in the field of dress fashion; and second, the problem of how this latter is worked out. It is worked out by departures from and assaults against the basic pattern of dress style, such as prevails in untense normal times. Where normality is at an extreme, whether this be an extreme of anatomy or of feasibility or wearability, movement is

22

toward the opposite extreme, whether that be a maximum or a minimum. Where normality of a dimension is at a median, tension movement is away from it toward either extreme. In all cases, what happens depends upon the quality of structure of the basic pattern when this is in "normal," that is, in relatively undisturbed condition. What the wars and revolutions do is to trigger disturbances in the stability of fashions. Wars and revolutions do not in themselves operate toward lengthening or shortening, widening or narrowing, raising or lowering any dimension of dress.

Nor would it be sound to assert that we had here an invariable law of history. In China or in ancient Rome, fashion sensitivity may have been much less responsive, its tempo far slower. Certainly the basic pattern was different there, and other dimensions of dress might have been affected than were affected in Europe, or possibly other features of dress than silhouette. Or again, the social classes observing change of fashion may have constituted a smaller segment of the population, or they may have been bound by sumptuary enactments, but insulated from effects of war and revolution; or war may have been too chronic a phenomenon to trigger new tensions. Each historic case has to be analyzed in its own terms—its own modes of war and revolutions, its own manners or basic structure of fashion. It would be the generic type of process that might be found to recur; it would not be expectable that sequences of specific events would repeat.

With these findings we have begun to touch on one

of the two main topics of our larger problem: the nature and role of civilizations, and their effects. Even more closely have we approached some of the fundamental problems of aesthetic styles in general: their changeability and developmental growth, what the nature of their coherence and permanence is, the attacks to which they are subject from within and without. Dress fashions obviously constitute a highly specialized species of art styles, sharing some of their generic qualities, unique in others. Dress fashions are also somewhat easier to analyze, especially quantitatively and objectively, than fine-art products; but some of their qualities we shall find recurring in the great styles of art.

The analysis has had at times to become finespun. From here on, I shall present no more statistics, not even in diagram. But I should like to outline a few generalities about fine-art styles, as a basis or platform on which to build up what I shall have to say in following chapters.

No one can doubt that there is such a thing as fine art, or pure art, and that it forms part of the totality of human social behavior or culture in the wider sense. Yet the boundaries of this province of fine art are not easy to draw with precision. Roughly, it will probably be agreed that where the element of creativity is predominant, we have fine-art products; where utility is the primary consideration, we are in applied arts, sometimes also called decorative arts. But as nothing completely pure is likely to exist very long in the imperfect world of reality, we must temper the implication of the name. Obviously, the artist mostly has to give regard to considerations of earning a living. His customer may be influenced more by motivations of display, luxury, social prestige than by genuinely aesthetic satisfaction as such. Many arts for both ear and eye have in their beginnings served religion as a mistress, and aimed at piety rather than beauty; some have never escaped this bondsman's role, or have sunk into it. However, our concern being not with precise definitions but with characteristic qualities, we may proceed to deal with the fine arts as if their identity had been formally established.

The fine arts vary among one another in the degree to which they represent or depict—as their products have a factual meaning or tell a story. Literature and much painting and sculpture do represent; though there are exceptions: most Islamic painting is nonrealistically decorative. Music and architecture, on the other hand, do not in themselves attempt representation, though they may tolerate a little of it as an adjunct. The representing arts thus possess a content, a subject matter, in addition to the form through which they express it. The nonrepresenting arts of music, architecture, decoration, and for the most part of dance deal directly with proportions or relations to one another of sounds, shapes, masses, colors, or movements, or relations of these to the composition as a whole. These arts have little subject matter independent of the expression of aesthetic form—the latter *is* their subject.

This generic difference has not prevented certain hybrid arts from developing, such as the opera; or for that matter, much theater contains dance, movement, costume, or decor in addition to the basic words of the dialogue.

Let us then without further preliminaries return to the construal of style as something concerned essentially with form, and possessing some consistency of the forms operated with; plus a coherence of these into a set of related larger patterns. And let us proceed from there.

It is universally accepted that the fine arts achieve values, and that these values continue to reside in products of the arts. These values afford certain peculiar pleasures, or perhaps better, satisfactions, which are distinct from utility satisfactions or the subsistence and maintenance of the act of living as such. These aesthetic satisfactions are sought as ends in themselves; though this fact does not prevent them from also getting associated and intertwined with other, nonaesthetic motivations.

It is also plain that aesthetic values reside primarily in the forms produced by art styles, rather than in the subject matter treated. This indeed is obvious in the case of nonrepresentative arts like music, which have no factual content. The conclusion might be extended from this case as a highly probable general principle holding for all the fine arts.

However, it may fairly be affirmed that to the layman, to the general public or average patron, the subject matter, where there can be one, ordinarily is important; perhaps more so than the form. The reverse holds for the artist. To him the form of the expression, even to the technique used, is the crux of his task; here lies his "creativity." The layman, unless specially educated, or self-trained, may be little aware of the form; his perception of it remains vague; he may know that he prefers this to that representation of the same subject, but he finds it difficult to say wherein the greater preferability or excellence lies; and he may take refuge in a generic unanalyzable quality, such as the mood produced in himself by a picture or poem. In children and the completely untutored, interest is centered almost wholly in the situation or act dealt with, in the scene per se, in the event and its outcome; and if one execution is preferred to another, it is likely to be because of greater clarity of delineation, or greater wealth of recognizable detail.

This broad difference of attitude, between the producers of representing art and the receivers of art, is one that must never be overlooked.

### NOTE ON SOURCES OF THE TABLES

Tables 1 and 2 are graphic conversions of part of the numerical data appearing in Tables 25 and 21 of A. L. Kroeber and Jane Richardson, "Three Centuries of Women's Dress Fashions: A Quantitative Analysis," *Univ. of California Pubs., Anthropological Records*, V, no. 2 (1940), 143, 139. Table 21 appears also in my *The Nature of Culture* (University of Chicago Press, 1952) as Table 2, p. 360. The fluctuation units there used are different from those shown in the present tables; and a diagram (fig. 7 of the original and fig. 9 of the republication) differs from the present graphic tables also in dealing with yearly variability instead of five-year means, as well as in the order of its columns. It must therefore not be confused with the present tables, although its general appearance and over-all significance are similar.

# 2

# Style in the Fine Arts

THERE remain a good many intriguing problems, not too clearly solved, in the matter of content and form in art. For instance, the difference between the madonnas of Leonardo, Perugino, Raphael, Titian—does that lie wholly in the sphere of creative form? Is each painter's distinctive visualization only that? Or is he also painting a different person? And how about the different feeling tone evoked by each?

In any event, there is in all works of representative art a third element, a certain technique or skill—brush strokes, choices of words, and such—through which the artist expresses what I have so far called creative "form," but which as technique can be distinguished from such form. It is the means of executing or achieving the form; it is part of a technical mastery or professional efficiency; and it is usually the last quality perceived by the spectator or layman, even when he may be emotionally aware of a quality of form.

We have then three ingredients of style in the representational fine arts. First is the gross or objective subject matter dealt with: whether it be a deity or a man that is shown, a figure in action or at rest, an animal or a view of nature, in the case of a picture; a sentiment, a happening, a clash, or a recollected image, in a poem.

Second is the "concept" of the subject, along with its emotional aura and its value toning. This is the factor that differentiates one portrait of a person from another painter's portrait of him, one poet's love longing or regret of death from another poet's. This is still, in one sense content, subject matter, but it is subjective content, as felt by the artist; and in another sense it is form, the product achieved by the artist and the style.

And third is the specific, technical form given the work of art by the artist in his execution of it—his diction, rhythm, or brush stroke. With this ingredient we have fully entered into the realm of creativity, of aesthetic achievement. This is the distinctive sphere of the artist himself. It is followed, *after the act,* by the critic, the connoisseur, the cultivated reader or viewer. They too react articulately to the creation; but secondarily or analytically. The untrained layman may experience interest, stir, admiration; he may actually know what he likes; but he mostly cannot "say" why he likes, not even particularize what it is that attracts him. His feeling may be strong as that of the smitten lover, but emotion makes him also dumb.

It would be possible to press farther, to go on from the brush stroke to the medium in which it is executed: whether the pigment is borne in water or tempera or oil, or frozen in glass, or abandoned in favor of the black and white of the engraver's point. To the artist, these considerations are all-important. They undoubtedly relate to his creativity. But they relate to it technically and technologically, as part of his virtuosity in both the good and the bad sense; and they bring us back in many cases to physical materials and their objective qualities, whether these materials be human vocal cords or the resonance of wood or the properties of marble as against clay, or of brush as against knife. Such considerations are important, but they are also highly special; and having recognized their existence, we must leave them in order to pursue our general interest in style.

For the nonrepresentational arts, such as music, the case is somewhat different, and seemingly simpler, because representation and the element of subject matter are to all intents lacking. On the other hand, the situation is also more complicated. For a creation in music to reach its maximum ultimate public, two creative artists are usually necessary: the composer and the performer. In principle, these apparently differ rather drastically; for while most notable composers have also been excellent performers or masters of performance, the reverse holds much less. The reason may be that, as such, the performer is reproducing, not originating. However, our purpose being not to differentiate the several fine arts from one another but to define the qualities of style as the arts possess these in common, we must leave this interesting bypath untrodden.

If the formation of a style is due to a series of creative acts, it is our third ingredient—execution, I have provisionally called it, for want of a better term—that is cardinal. This fact can hardly be emphasized sufficiently. Especially must a corollary or implication of it be kept always in mind. Aesthetic execution is a specialized and co-ordinated selection from among a variety of possible expressions; and the expressions of the artists living in one region and period—in the same tradition, in short—are highly interrelated and co-ordinated, even if they may also be highly individuated. In fact, this interrelation of their modes of expression (or executions) is what makes a style, in the social sense of the word. A historical style can be defined as the co-ordinated pattern of interrelations of individual expressions or executions in the same medium or art.

This interdependence obviously is one-way because it occurs in the flow of time, and only predecessors or contemporaries can influence successors. To this must be added a fact that is less patent and that has again and again been overlooked, namely, that predecessors *must* influence successors. Even when their effect is negative, it serves as a stimulant. The take-off for a variation in execution is always the already traversed course of the style, or some part or facet of it; it is never actually a "return to nature," never a wholly fresh observing of the objective world by the uncontaminated mind of individual genius, as enthusiasm so often proclaims it to be. The testimony of artists on this point is not always credible. They may focus with such keen intensity on how they differ from their predecessors that they see only the difference, and may talk as if they had invented their differentiation out of nothing. But a judicial analysis of the course of development of any art belies such a belief. Beyond this, fine arts are among the flowerings of cultures, all of which are social growths in the channels of traditions.

André Malraux in his *Voices of Silence* has re-emphasized this point. The artist has been conditioned from the start of his career by the paintings or statues he has seen. He has seen them differently from other men: that is why he is an artist, and they are not. They see nature, and nothing comes of it, beyond perhaps moods; he sees nature as previous artists have remodeled it in their executions. It is these predecessors' *expression* of nature—their art—that triggers him into imitating them, and, if he happens to possess the energy, imagination, and skill, to transcend them. It is not nature that breeds art but art that breeds art. Nature is merely the inexhaustible reservoir into which the artist dips, to take out what the state of tradition of his art, plus his individual personality in the ban of that tradition, tell him to select and use.

Malraux says that "it is never the sheep that inspire a Giotto, but rather his first sight of paintings" of them.

He points out that no painter progresses "directly from his drawings as a child to the work of his maturity. Artists do not stem from their childhood, but from their conflict with the achievements of their predecessors." They struggle with the forms which other artists have "imposed on life." All painters and sculptors begin by imitating others. They begin not with a sudden uprush of emotion taking form in a void, but with sensing the form-expressed emotion of another artist.

If this holds in painting, sculpture, and literature which operate through representations of life and nature, it is evidently true also of essentially nonrepresentational arts like music, dance, architecture.

All the foregoing we can infer as fact from unprejudiced scrutiny of the biographies of artists. But it greatly invigorates the concept of traditional arts as being fundamentally social growths—cultural processes resulting in cultural products. And let us note, in this connection, how difficult it is to name great artists in any art who stand historically isolated, who had no contemporary artists, no near predecessors in their homelands. Goya, perhaps? or François Villon? But Goya worked long in Italy; and Villon wrote in verse forms centuries old.

Any art rising from obscurity to its first modest achievements has to make certain choices and therewith commitments; and as its condition develops farther, momentum increases, and it is usually more profitable to improve, refine, extend these commitments than to start all over again with contrary or unrelated choices. If poetry has begun, as in Greece, with measuring lengths of syllables in lines, additional variants of quantitative syllable patterns of line and stanza are likely to be developed. Therewith there tends to be increasingly inhibited any rise of mere syllable counting as in the Romance languages, or patterning of stress accents as in English, or rhyming as it was first devised in China. Here we are right in the crucial aesthetic ingredient of the execution or technique of achieving form; but subject matter, medium, and the emotional value sought for may also be highly selective.

Similarly, a musical style may start with melody, rhythm, and timbre differentiation, but never attain to harmony. It may commit itself to a scale of fairly wide and even-spaced notes, such as we call pentatonic; or again, to one in which the intervals vary between quite wide and very narrow ones—of semitone or less. Whatever the scale commenced with, it becomes increasingly difficult to abandon as the art progresses. The frame helps strongly to channel the course of development.

Many art styles accordingly follow a course not unlike the trajectory of a missile—with a definite rise and fall, and persisting at least more or less in one general direction. This is particularly true of arts that have grown up in national or regional isolation—as most styles in past known history have grown: their trajectories have had few influences from outside to disturb their course.

From this again flows the comparability of stages of growth evident in so many unconnected art styles. There is crude stiffness or ineptitude at the emergence; an archaic phase with form developing into definiteness but still rigid; then the freeing from archaism, followed by a rapid culmination of the style with full achievement of the potentialities for plasticity inherent in it; after which there may come a straining for effect, overexpressionism, or again ultrarealism, or a flamboyant rococo or over-ornamentation; if indeed repetitive atrophy of form—a veritable death of feeling in the style—has not preceded these latter. Most of the terms descriptive of these successive phases—archaic, flamboyant, rococo—are taken from the history of European sculpture and architecture, but are applicable in India or China, in Egypt or aboriginal Mexico also; and in part they fit recognizable phases in styles of painting, music, and literature.

It is an old saying that while civilization as a whole progresses with time, the great arts soon wither away and have to begin all over again. There is considerable truth in this view. Practically useful knowledge is not likely to be forgotten, especially once writing exists to hand it along. Inventions are rarely lost altogether, even if their use may be abandoned through lack of resources in times of economic disaster. That whole part of civilization which is concerned with survival and subsistence and welfare must in its nature face reality. Means once achieved are accordingly likely to be retained and added to. So the general course of this practical component of civilization is cumulative. But the fine arts face values, not reality, and do not grow cumulatively; or at least they have not generally grown cumulatively through their recorded history. So they come in intermittent spurts instead of going on continuously. It is not too clear what determines where their development stops, except that it seems to be the point at which the values—or ideals, if one like—that are shaped as the art grows have been attained by the artists' execution, and therewith are exhausted. Unless the goals can now be set farther ahead or widened, and the style be reconstituted on a new basis, there is nothing left for its practitioners but maintenance of the status reached; which is in its nature—by implied definition, as it were—incompatible with the play of creative activity. In other words, styles are produced by forces that are inherently dynamic. It is difficult for styles to become static without deteriorating or disintegrating. The developmental flow of style is one of its most characteristic qualities.

What happens to a style after it has reached its realization or exhaustion point—realization of its ideals, exhaustion of its potentialities—what happens to it from then on is quite variable in detail. The style deteriorates, but the ways of deterioration are multiple.

Where the style is relatively simple but highly defined, consistent but limited in its goals, and content with its goals, and forbidden by religion or a strong conserving cast of the civilization to attempt enlargement of these goals, as in ancient Egyptian sculpture and painting, then a simple freezing of manner and quality of performance is possible. But let the conditions of life in the society slip downward, with weakening of political administration, economic worsening, or other insecurity, and the art promptly shows deterioration. It becomes slovenly, hasty, inaccurate or inelegant in line, uses baser material, and applies laxer technique to it, and poor finish. But let political and economic functioning regain effectiveness, and the art reacquires its pristine qualities, and returns almost identically to its former canons. Three times did Egyptian art return essentially to the style and quality of its original culmination in the fourth and fifth dynasties of the Old Kingdom: in the twelfth, the eighteenth, and the twenty-sixth dynasties—the Middle Kingdom, the New Empire, and the Late Renaissance. To be sure, the style of these several periods scattered through two thousands years is not absolutely identical. But it is essentially identical: even a novice can identify all the phases as Egyptian and never confound any of them with any non-Egyptian style. The expert, familiar with differential minutiae, can tell the periods apart, but even he is likely to note first the divergences in content, in subject matter represented, such as changes in the dress worn, or that when horses are depicted we are in the New or the Late Empires, the Old and Middle Kingdoms having known only the native ass.

In fact the totality of ancient Egyptian civilization underwent much more change in these two thousand years than did its art. Wheels, iron, new domestic animals were introduced from abroad along with new materials and new inventions, and other inventions were made at home. The consequence was that from 2600 to 600 B.C. the totality of life and culture altered at hundreds of points, while Egyptian art stood almost still. Here was a figurative and symbolic art which, contrary to the rule that styles flow, froze contentedly and repeatedly back to its first culmination, whereas in the actual and practical business of carrying on his life the Egyptian slowly admitted innumerable innovations. It is evident that when they so wish, people can hold their ideal outlook, their art and religion, as the most nearly constant part of their universe.

It is of interest that Egyptian art showed one single inclination from within to alter its course, as contrasted with the declines to which it was subject from politico-economic causes. This happened under the famous heretic king, the monotheist Akhnaton, toward the close of the most successful of all dynasties, the eighteenth, when power, wealth, and art were all in culmination. Militarily and abroad, a decline had indeed just begun, though it can hardly have yet been much felt in Egypt itself. The attempt to change was thus seemingly prompted rather by a surplus of energy, a surfeit of success, an exploratory and expansive national mood. Or let us say, a royal mood, the mood of a royal entourage, with national resources adequate to sustain considerable innovation. At bottom, the monotheistic episode may stem, as alleged, from an endeavor by the dominant court faction to limit the power of a hampering or encroaching priesthood. At any rate, whether the first motivation was factional or intellectual, it was corporate religion that was attacked, and a new philosophy and worship were endorsed and proclaimed by the divine king. This monotheistic reform failed with the king's early death; but with it went a movement, which remained largely successful, to modernize writing and perhaps style of literature, and another to make formal art more naturalistic. To us today the gain in attempted truthfulness of art representation appears rather small. We see a slightly different conventional canon substituted for the old one, with possibly a naturalistic touch or two introduced as a compliment to royal physique. In any event, the new philosophy and art alike collapsed with Akhnaton's death, and left no apparent trace of influence on the subsequent course of philosophy, ritual, or art. It is in accord with what we know of the comportment of Egyptian art elsewhere through its history, that this attempted innovation of the style did not arise primarily within the art, among the sculptors and painters, so far as we can tell, but was imposed upon them by power above; though some of the artists may have been willing or eager to meet the change.

At any rate, the over-all course of art in ancient Egypt, though its rise seems to have been rapid and a true flow, once it had reached its goal, was used by the masters of the civilization, secular and religious, as an instrument for conservation of the culture as it was. Religion has apparently been utilized far more often and more successfully in history than art as such a conserving tool.

Let us consider the declines of some other art styles.

Greek sculpture, of which on account of its partial preservation we have much fuller knowledge than of Greek painting, culminated between Pericles and Alexander. It continued for several centuries at a less eminent level, though still an effective art, influential westward through Roman dominion and eastward to India. Perhaps the first phase after Praxiteles was one of expressionism—expression of emotion and effort, dynamic and strained, sometimes contorted. A comparison with the baroque sculpture of Bernini after Donatello and Michelangelo is pertinent, and the time interval was about the same as from Praxiteles to the friezes of Pergamum. The Laocoön and Niobe are other examples. An overlapping phase was naturalism, associated with genre subjects and with a more realistic portraiture than was attempted in the great period. This realism became a specialty of Roman sculpture, with a subculmination of its own early in the second century of the Empire. A third tendency faced away from these two, back to the great golden past, and was therefore avowedly academic and derivative, sometimes deliberately archaizing—Neo-Attic. In fine, Hellenic sculpture, which became Graeco-Roman, was split into several currents, plus transitions, and much eclecticism. The appropriate metaphor is that of a great river entering its delta.

The third and fourth centuries of our era, when Graeco-Roman art rapidly declined into coarseness, especially in the West, were also the period of the spread and success of Christianity. The new religion had new themes to be portrayed, but having no stock of visual expressions of its own, of necessity took over the established classical forms. Between the worsening of technique that was already in progress, the stripping off of pagan elements, and the greater interest of the converts in their new beliefs than in the form in which these were expressed—because of these combining influences, the old style which had begun as Hellenic art now sank to levels of crudity it had not dipped to in a thousand years. At the same time this early Christian art, with its new orientation, was laying the foundations of what was to become "Western" or "European" sculpture and painting. Its very amorphousness made possible a development in new directions, which could hardly have occurred had the old Classical Mediterranean style maintained more of its hold, strength, and skill. This is shown by what happened in the Eastern or Byzantine half of the realm where Greek language, culture, and art were more deeply rooted and the empire was preserved. The art here also of course became Christian, and with an ascetic, monastic, and severe cast, but with far more preservation of a sense of the old aesthetic forms and standards than in the broken, tumultuous, ungoverned, and barbarized West. Byzantine art may truly be said to have mainly atrophied and fossilized repetitively, whereas Western Roman art disintegrated. Yet the very barbarization of Western art enabled it gradually to evolve new patterns of style—Romanesque, Gothic, Renaissance—and to achieve a great culmination of its own after a thousand years, when petrified Greek art had crumbled away with the Byzantine empire.[1]

Like the realm and culture centered at Constantinople, Byzantine art remained bound in the fetters of its past.

---

[1] A dash of Byzantine influence entered early Renaissance art, and was followed by the effect of discoveries of ancient monuments in Italy, but the great Renaissance culmination was of course mainly autonomous and original, not a reawakening or return.

The West, having lost most of the civilization it once had, floundered and moiled for centuries but gradually forged for itself a new future.

Political revolutions are often fought for ideals, but always involve also overturning of power and wealth to new hands. Such transfers are hardly possible in aesthetic revolutions, although ego assertions can play a part. In the main, however, revolutions in style, whether successful or unsuccessful, seem to arise when there is a sense that the existing style has exhausted its possibilities; that most of what can be done with its forms and techniques has been done; and that the future of present executants is therefore being cramped by the hold of the past: genuinely creative impluses are frustrated when their outlets are mainly reduced to repetition. There may still remain certain new themes and new mannerisms to be discovered conformable to the existing style, or extending it. But when these have been found and established, original imagination faces a dead end. Unwilling to accept resignation, imagination may fight.

If there is still room for some change within the style, a battle for dominance may take place, as when toward 1830 the romantics revolted in French art and literature, and won, only to be superseded in their turn within a few decades by naturalism and impressionism. When the smoke had cleared from the romantic battle, and still more in further retrospect, the freedoms gained seemed somewhat trivial as against the heat with which the revolution had been staged. There was a change, but the courses of both literature and art visibly have remained continuous in France: there was no sudden break at any point, not even a sharp angle in the road traveled.[2]

In time, however, the romantic movement and its heirs were subjected to attacks by genuinely revolutionistic programs—indeed, anarchistic ones, which set out to abolish all rule of style. Verse was to be "free," that is formless, and representative arts nonrepresentative: cubist, abstractionist, nonobjective. Nor were the arts to be allowed refuge in mere decoration, which normally moves with balance, symmetry, and repetition. In fact, there was to be abolition of all previous aesthetic order. There is no doubt that these movements aimed at an outright disruption of the basic patterns of European art styles as they had evolved over many centuries.

It is perhaps extreme to attribute these events wholly to exhaustion of existent style patterns. Politicoeconomic unsettlements may have furnished both stimulus and example. And a vastly larger public, for the first time touched somewhat by higher education and art, but still with unschooled taste, may have contributed. But the effects of the movements, if successful, would certainly have been the total leveling of all the aesthetic styles of our civilization. And inasmuch as the origination and leadership of the anarchic movements was throughout

[2] In German literature, where romanticism came both earlier and with more uncalculated vehemence, its effects were perhaps equally blurry, but this was so because the existing style that was reacted against was much more recently and less firmly established. There was in fact a protoromanticism nearly half a century earlier—labeled "Storm and Stress"—whose chief stylistic quality was a heightened tension of expression.

by writers, painters, sculptors, and musicians and not by politicians or Marxists, we are driven to conclude that the dominant causation was presumably internal to the arts. Whether this means that the potentialities of the styles had actually been exhausted; or whether personalities arose that felt the opportunities left them were insufficiently great; or how far the frustrated were ready for any overturn (and there were leaders eager for any following)—these are alternative possibilities that should be considered.

It is also pertinent that all the assaults contained as an essential element some innovating mode of technique of execution of works of art—the meter of poems, the brush strokes of paintings, the scale or system of consonance of music—in addition to the new themes proclaimed as mandatory. In painting, this had begun to happen well before the frontal efforts to disintegrate style: already with the impressionists nearly a century ago. Outline was to be broken up; not the object was to be painted, but its lighting or impression; not its surface, but the atmosphere between it and the beholder; from which it was only a step to suppress representation of things in favor of representations of space. These impressionist efforts of the later nineteenth century were not yet attempts to wreck the style as a whole; rather were they efforts to alter the style by emphasizing possibilities that had until then been neglected. But as the emphasis on the novelties grew heavier, older elements tended to recede and fade out, with the result that as the manner became more extreme and one-sided, more and more of the previous style had *de facto* been eliminated. This perhaps in some minds cultivated tolerance toward the idea of total elimination, of a complete doing away with all the past of the art. At any rate, it is clear that the effective alterations were made by artists within the art, in fulfillment of their personalities, not at behest of outside theorists. Also, the innovators were not incompetents unable to achieve in the established tradition—though their imitators might often be inept and merely mannered. The innovators indeed might have had a more immediately comfortable success if they had conformed to tradition; but their ultimate rating and fame would in that case presumably have been lower. It is also interesting that when the coherent force of the impressionist group movement was spent, and its members rutted farther and farther into their personal channels, and the neoimpressionists took over, it was again matters of technique that were in the forefront—the myriad dots of pointillist Seurat, the vehement swirls of raised pigment by Van Gogh.

In literature the career of Joyce is equally illustrative of the general principles we are considering. He started conventionally enough with some adequate but undistinguished poetry, and with *Dubliners*, a collection of stories, of which the last attained to a climax of extraordinary poignancy. One such passage however hardly justified much expectation of a really outstanding career by mere perseverance, and Joyce turned off to exile, to his *Portrait of the Artist as a Young Man*, to *Ulysses*, and to *Finnegans Wake*, to poverty, obscurity, and obloquy from much of the world for his remaining years, though he was also the great champion of a growing following, perhaps most numerous after his death. By the time his manner was fully developed, it had dispensed with objective events, with grammar and sentences, often with meaning in terms of English, and had substituted introspection, a coined vocabulary, and an infinite play of free-associational punning. There are those who hold this a supreme achievement, the founding of a new literature, and others who see in it only stubbornly perverse egotism carried to a simulation of psychopathology. What can perhaps be agreed to by nearly all is that Joyce's final style is an ultrapersonal one, dispensing both with narrative manner and with English, in favor of samples of the working of his own inner mind and of a language designed by and for himself. I am not in the least questioning Joyce's ability in what he chose to do. But he was substituting for the tradition of English prose narrative style as it had been developed over the centuries, the private style of James Joyce, as personal as he could make it in both preoccupation and expression. It was in short an attack upon all the past of his art. In this endeavor to destroy a great style, to substitute himself for a national and cultural tradition, lies the historic significance of James Joyce.

There is this to be said for the attempt: that a higher structure requires a wider base; and that there come times when in order to build greatly it may be more advisable to raze entirely and erect afresh. Thus the collapse of Minoan civilization left some centuries of Dark Age in Greece, but made possible the development of a broader and richer Greek civilization. Most of us also feel that Western culture is a greater construct than was the Hellenic or Graeco-Roman one; and it may be that this larger construct could not have been made had there not been a new religion and new barbarian forces and internal convulsions to topple the old. Perhaps five hundred years of Dark Age confusion and barbarism were needed to make possible the replacement of Greek art, science, and philosophy and Roman Empire and law by their broader Western counterparts. Not of course that Joyce singlehanded can do what it took Christianity, Goths, Vandals, and Franks several centuries to accomplish. But if he prove a precursor or symptom of similar destructive currents, precedent suggests that the ultimate outcome may be a larger reconstruction.

Much as there ensues confusion when the period of supreme strength of an empire has ended, be it that of Alexander, of Rome, of Charlemagne, we have seen that there is confusion when an important and coherent style has passed its zenith. There ensues a pulling in different directions—some groups plunging on ahead, some pulling back uphill, others trying to stand still or to edge sideways. Sometimes the divergent impulses may be active in a single personality. At any rate we have a contemporary case in perhaps our greatest living painter: Pablo Picasso. A somewhat similar case of unreconciled impulses in literature might be made for Goethe; but on the whole his phases were more successive. He passed on from one stage to another, where lesser men only deepened one characteristic execution. Picasso, however, has vibrated between his blue and circus manners, his neoclassic, the cubistic, the wholly abstract, the super-symbolic of Guernica and Minotauromachy, and with essentially equal intensity and success in each. It is true that there has been some drift with age toward greater leaning to the symbolic, but it has been accompanied by return to the other manners, and experimenting in new ones. We have here the unusual phenomenon of a great talent extremely sensitive to the first stirrings of new substyles, and able to switch his several powers into their full development, splitting himself aesthetically into alternant multiple personalities.

There is another feature of art styles that is character-istic of contemporary days, in fact is peculiar to them. Heretofore, no style—and no civilization—has ever pre-vailed over more than a minor fraction of this planet's surface. Many styles, great and small, were always flour-ishing simultaneously. Mostly the artists following them did not even know of the existence of most of the other styles. Here and there there might be interinfluences, but they were not too common or too deep, and most styles in most arts through most of history have grown up autonomously and in essential insulation. If foreign influences had a hand in the formation of a style, this was soon forgotten, and by the time it approached maturity, its practitioners no longer knew or were interested in the former alien impingements. It is doubtful whether Phidias knew enough of the history of incipient Greek sculpture to be aware of its absorptions from Crete and Egypt and Asia.

Now, however, two factors have changed this normal condition under which hitherto the arts have been practiced by the human species. The first is the shrinkage of our planet by the mushrooming growth of intercommunications. The second is the fact that at least the visual arts of the whole world, including many past arts, have been gathered in museums, spread by photography and reproduction, and are available to, nay, knocking at the doors of, our ateliers and living rooms. This second factor is preconditioned by the first, that of greater intercommunication; but its specific ingredient is the fact that our aesthetic lives are now lived as it were in the illumination of a world museum instead of the candlelighting, as heretofore, of a national or uniregional art. No visual art can henceforth wholly escape being influenced by the totality of the arts of mankind. Malraux has made this fact clear again in his *Voices of Silence*. In the presence of this unheard-of degree of impingement, there is already greater receptivity, and this is bound to grow. True, there will also no doubt be efforts at stylistic isolationism, and some of these will be locally and temporarily successful. But in proportion as they are successful, they will reaffect style in the larger open world, and thereby a new interrelation will be established which will feed back the influences from the larger styles to the regional ones. All this means that there is genuine prospect of the visual arts of the human race henceforth entering into a condition of unresolved coexistence, of eddies and currents within one larger stream, of an uneasy schizoidness foreshadowed by Picasso's multiple stylistic personality.

There surely are elements of danger in such a condition. But we need not yield wholly to fears. Resoluteness in meeting the situation may reveal unexpected new potentialities. Eclecticism has in the past normally been a symptom of flagging of positive originality in the artist, or in the stage of the style of which he formed part; its products run much risk of being an elegant but characterless mishmash. But the point is that we shall no longer be able to infer the future from the past to the degree that has been valid heretofore: from now on, the whole history of styles promises to contain new factors that will produce new courses of events. No one can accuse Picasso of being indecisive in execution, of weakness; he is highly original, and he is supremely skilled, even if his art is split stylistically. If his single personality can contain several styles without mishmashing them—as Goethe already successfully expressed ultraromanticism and Hellenic classicism side by side—surely a world art should be able to contain them. The weaker practitioners will blend and fudge and eclecticize; but they will have less influence and be soon forgotten. The stronger ones will not only be able to manage multiple manners, but the essence of their creativity is likely to lie in the contrast they feel and can achieve between these manners. We shall have, in that event, something new in the world: a style that is comparative instead of exclusive, and conscious instead of ignorant of universal art history. There will be great risks, but exciting possibilities.

Let me pour this much oil on the troublous waters of this envisioning. Great changes do not happen overnight. If this one does happen, it will take time and come gradually. Also, there is no reason to believe that every artist will be driven to eclecticize or learn to juggle. The majority will quite likely continue successfully to cultivate one manner in which they were born or educated, or which they have chosen as the one most compatible to their personal skill and likings, leaving the comparison and wider contrastive activity to the art as a whole, or to those personalities in it that are irresistibly attracted by the severalty of its sides.

Another qualification is that this prospect of merging of all regional and national styles into one universal but multiple style may not offhand be assumed to hold equally for all the arts. The prospect is certainly much the strongest for the visual arts which produce material objects, objects which can and sometimes do withstand the centuries, and can be further preserved in museums. We know that the surviving Greek and Roman sculpture had something of such an influence in Europe at occasional spots even during the Middle Ages, more in the Renaissance, and again after the rediscovery of Pompeii and before the rise of neoclassicism. They exercised another such influence in the early Christian centuries through Buddhist Gandhara that extended as far as China and Japan. But we cannot trace anything comparable for

Greek and Roman music. Melodies are intangible; archaeology cannot recover them; and all indications are that no outright flow of music comparable to that of Greek sculpture ever did take place westward and eastward. If we are to have a universal style in music, it will not be through any digging up and assembling, but through movements of people, contacts, hearing, and learning from music performances—all of which would at best yield a somewhat different situation from that I have projected for the visual arts.

For literature, we have still another set of conditions. Writing does preserve extinct literatures. Translation spreads them—almost without loss so far as they consist of prose, inadequately for form of verse, but substantially for theme. And languages can be and are learned. Yet there are contrary factors which would tend to impede universalization: above all languages are numerous, and poetic forms must fit the properties of their languages. The quantitative prosody of Greek could be transferred to Latin which also distinguished long vowels from short, and could arise in Arabic for the same reason. It cannot be used in Chinese nor in modern English, in both of which length is not present phonemically—the so-called long and short syllables of English really differing only qualitatively. And the quantitative meters repeatedly "introduced" by English—and French—poets are essentially self-delusions under the influence of the way these speakers of languages mispronounced Latin. Similarly it will be evident that it would be impossible to transfer to phonemically nontonal languages, as most

European ones are, the tone-arrangement patterns which characterize much of post-T'ang Chinese verse.

True, some features of language, though not many, are universal. One could presumably count syllables in all languages, also find rhyming words. However, even here there are differences, sometimes between closely related languages. Two-syllable rhymes are prevalent in Italian, because the language "gives" them—the normal stress falls on the second syllable from the end. French calls them feminine rhymes and alternates them with masculine one-syllable rhymes, which is easy because all the many French words ending in a "mute-*e*" syllable are natural feminine rhymes. German also has a mute or weak-stressed *e* frequent in final position, so natural feminine rhymes abound, and they are used almost as often as in French. English, however, has lost the pronunciation of these unstressed final syllables—Chaucer still pronounced them, and that is what makes it hard for us to scan him—so that the number of naturally given feminine rhymes is quite small in modern English. They often have to be made up of two words, and in general are somewhat contrived and tours de force. These differences are thus inherent in the languages, and will remain effective in them until the languages change. They are in no sense due to the "soul" of English and of French poesy wanting different expressions: the "soul" rather is afforded or denied certain mechanisms of expression by the language; but, once habituated, the soul—if there is one—flatters itself that it has sought and found its perfect vehicle.

All this will suggest some notion of why a world-wide style in literature will encounter greater difficulties than in the visual arts. The nearest approach to something universal is by a happening that has occurred several times in history on a subcontinental scale and that now seems conceivable on a supercontinental and global basis. Chinese, Sanskrit, Arabic, Greek, Latin have all at one time become the dominant language of a large international civilization—through conquest or through sheer cultural supremacy or both. Underneath these great and widespread languages of culture, particular nations retained their national idiom for familiar and native use. They spoke it as a vernacular, perhaps also wrote it; but greater matters were written, and formally spoken, in the language of higher culture. All this has taken place before, and may take place again, but on a world-wide basis. It seems a more likely event than the establishment of any artificial or synthetic universal language, or than the gradual assimilation of all existing languages to a point where their literatures will be freely transferable.

Such are some of the generic properties of aesthetic styles, and some of the problems arising from them.

# 3

# Style and Civilizations

IT IS time to discuss certain broad problems of styles and their bearing on civilizations in history. There is first the relation of style to genius, and considerations raised by this. Then there is the question of how far stylelike qualities can be recognized in cultural activities other than art—say science; and here I have a partly positive answer to give. Next there is the problem of whether or how far civilizations as wholes may profitably be conceived as having some of the properties of styles, either in their nature or in their historical behavior. I shall only broach this: in one form or another, problems of civilization will occupy the remainder of the book. Finally, I want to suggest that analogues of certain qualities of style can be detected in some segments of nature lying far outside the bounds of human activities, namely, in the forms of life itself. And this view will involve a bit of philosophizing on how the immediacy of our knowledge affects the course of science and our understanding of civilizations as against understanding of individuals.

As for the relation of style to genius, a degree of connection would probably be accepted by everyone. The readiest response might be: yes, the great men make the style, especially what is best in it. And, indeed, it is their work that largely constitutes the style, particularly what the future will remember of it. Another answer might be socially oriented, and would see a style as a continuing historic event, in which the great men—and the lesser ones as well—appear as points in the movement of the flow. "Links in the chain of the style" might be a trite but more concrete and less accurate metaphor; "positions in the progress of its curve," a more mathematical rendering of the situation.

There is no conflict between these several statements. In a matter-of-fact and common-sense way, a style consists of the products of the men associated with the style. They make the style, literally and unquestionably. When we are operating biographically, when the interest is in individual personalities and their workings, we need nothing more. The style is only background for the person who has the spotlight of interest on him. But the more the interest is historic, and broadly or comparatively historic, the less do individual idiosyncracies matter as against the course of the style as a whole. It is not that the persons involved are now denied, but that attention has shifted to a larger movement that extends beyond the individualities. It is the interrelations of the persons that count now, rather than the persons in themselves. The objective lens of our mental microscope has been moved farther away, the individual is *no longer* in focus, a larger field *is* in focus, and what is in clear sight in this field is the total configuration and the interrelation of its parts.

The Romans, who lived within the same civilization as the Greeks but enough later for them to have perspective on the Greeks—these ancients already realized that great names do not occur studded evenly over history but in concentrations, like constellations in the sky. Most especially is this apparent in the fine arts, where styles hold sway. The three great tragedians of antiquity lived at Athens within a century, then had no equals in the rest of antiquity—in fact no peers in two thousand years. Where else is there a burst of absolute top-flight painters comparable to those of the Italian Renaissance? A dozen years ago, in *Configurations of Culture Growth*, I devoted several hundred pages to collecting instances of this sort and setting them forth in detail. By the time I ended, I was impressed by the fewness of instances of first-rank artists, in any art, standing outside a constellation, randomly alone. I believe that any one else who will seriously concern himself with similar data of his own assembling, or who will trouble himself to redigest mine, will come to the same conclusion. When once we center interest in the interrelations instead of the individuals, these latter certainly lose their independence and appear as members of configurations. In one sense, men make a style; in another sense, they are themselves its products.

At any rate, I emerged from this preoccupation with some unorthodox notions about genius. I do agree that genius consists of a special capacity very much above average human capacity, or of several such abilities, possibly at times of a rather all-round heightening of capacities. I also assume, with perhaps every one else, that such powers are congenitally based. This being so, we should expect births of individuals with genius capacity to occur more or less evenly, with probability of random scatter—one in ten thousand, one in a million, whatever the rate may be, according as we set the criterion of genius lower or higher. This would certainly be expectable within any given race during the longish period within which it could be presumed not to alter its genetic constitution appreciably. There would further be at least some presumption of this even rate holding even as between separate races, or until it shall have been shown— as it has not been—that races differ in ability.

Of course achieved capacity as manifested in life must be distinguished from potential capacity as it comes to us by heredity. A true mathematical genius of highest potential, born into an environment where no one counted above a hundred, would not invent the calculus or a theory of numbers, nor would he even discover geometry or algebra; though he might achieve a method of performing simple multiplication. My point is simply a large-scale application of the principle contained in this illustration. Granted that gifts are individually congenital, it is the cultural setting into which they are born that makes or prevents their realization. I computed that even in the greater civilizations of history, with their rich and varied settings, when their more and their less productive periods are taken together, there must be at least three-fourths, perhaps nine-tenths of their potential geniuses that never come to flowering for posterity to recognize. And if we take the whole human population through its whole history, including conditions alike of great and of lesser civilization, of semicivilization, of barbarism and primitivism all together, then the percentage of realization of genius is of course even less, possibly only 2 or 3 per cent.

It sounds like a terrible indictment of human culture. It is; until we realize that without culture the percentage would have been zero. If the charge against human culture be amended to read that it is as yet a very imperfect instrument, I am in entire agreement.

In general, we all recognize genius in intellectual pursuits as fully as in the arts. Moreover, it is clear that geniuses come in clusters in philosophy and science much as they do in poetry, drama, music, painting, and sculpture. However there is one important difference from the arts in the historical behavior of science. At first blush, science seems to go on cumulatively irrespective of period, and even from one civilization to another. One period of science can begin where another left off, it is generally believed. The arts, however, always seem to have to begin all over again, as we have said before. At any rate they do largely begin over, and they mostly borrow but little from the arts of other civilizations. Some accumulation may take place, but it is certainly not a typical or conspicuous process in art history generally.

I suggest that this double-facedness or differential between science and the arts is due to an ambiguity in our popular concept of science, and that analysis shows science to contain two components, or groups of components, one of which is more and the other less akin to art.

The difference between the two components lies principally in their motivation. If the primary interest is in understanding, as such, as an end in itself, without afterthought of utility or profit, the course of science runs much like that of the arts. It comes in bursts or pulses, each dedicated to a particular set of problems. As these problems become solved by the methods and the point of view available, novel or profound results become fewer, and the science slackens, except for quantity of detailed findings. It is only with the discovery of a new orientation, like twentieth-century genetics or subatomic structure, that discoveries of originality and transcendent importance are once again made, and a new burst of geniuses occurs. The new interpretations are accumulative in the sense that they do not sweep away all that was previously known. The old data are supplemented by new ones of more poignant significance; but mostly they are not abolished or discarded: they are reinterpreted, given more meaning. Yet the front of crucial activity—

creative activity—has changed, and it runs its own course anew. This is the way I see fundamental or pure science progressing, and it is not too different a way from development in the arts.

I had started to say "theoretical science" here, but I hesitate, because of a current false dichotomy which separates science into a higher layer of theory and a lower layer of information on phenomena. Such a dichotomy is likely to encourage a logicoverbal virtuosity as sterile as is mere fact-collecting. In truly successful fundamental science, theory, method, and data are not stratified into a caste system but are integrated on one functional level.

The second main component of science is that which thinks primarily of the useful, whether that be the alleviating of ill health, or technological advance, or practical inventions, or the increase of production or of savings in cost or time. This utilitarian component must not be looked on as in any way inferior to the other component of science. I expressly do not wish to make that value judgment. But the behavior of the utilitarian component, as we look back over history, is different. It is largely accumulative. A practical gain is not going to be forgotten or given up unless to a similar but further improved innovation. And through the inclination toward technology, and the affiliation of this with economy and industry, applied science is likely to develop in a more even, less pulsating course than pure science.

This finding is confirmed by history. The great age of Greek mathematics, physics, and astronomy was not accompanied by any marked progress in technology. On the other hand the inventions in harness and saddles which multiplied the efficiency of the horse, the deep-turning plows with moldboard, the increasing spread of watermills and origin of windmills, the use of these natural powers for more than mealing grain and their first application in mills for crushing, fulling, and sawing, the development of gear-driven clocks and of artillery, the invention of spectacles and of printing—all these, beginning almost within the Dark Ages, precede the burst of European science that commenced with Copernicus and Galileo. From Archimedes and Hipparchus to Copernicus is more than a millennium and a half of exceedingly slow movement in fundamental science, but the last half of the arid interval was filled by notable technological progress. Thus quite evidently the two principal components of science move through history with less reference to each other than the relation of the intellectual strand to fine art, of the utilitarian strand to technology and industry.

If pure science then shows one behavioral relationship to the fine arts, the question arises whether there are others, whether there might be in science indications of styles more or less comparable to those that are so essential a property of the arts. First reaction is likely to be negative to this suggestion, on the ground that science deals with uncovering the truth of reality, which is supposed to be one and fixed, whereas styles vary optionally. Even if an art represents nature, it may be argued, fidelity is only one of its aims, and often a secondary one. However, psychologists have become increasingly aware that perception is not merely a sort of mechanical reflex of reality, but that we perceive according to our "set"—the congenital, conditioned, habitual way we are triggered. And concepts tend to follow percepts, but at the same time also slant them further. Certainly two distinct civilizations would influence their members both to perceive and conceive nature somewhat differently.

If it be countered that the business of science is to penetrate beyond these subjective conditionings to the unalterable objective reality behind them, that is no doubt true; but it is only an already sophisticated science, skilled in experiment and equipped with precision instruments, that can hope to penetrate beyond. In its beginnings, all science must carry a fairly heavy load of conditioning, and here the greatest variety of diverse manners and styles would show both in the conduct and in the results of science.

So far as I know, this idea, that science shares at least a degree of the relativity that is characteristic of all human culture, was first realized by Spengler. At any rate, he definitely made the point, although as usual he greatly overstated it. That he asserted it most fully for mathematics is perhaps natural, since mathematics, being free of phenomenal content, is in a sense a more nearly untrammeled intellectual activity than the remainder of science, and therefore more visibly conditioned by the matrix of its particular culture. However, with his profoundly monadal point of view, Spengler was bound to see separate cultures producing totally diverse sciences, and he cites instances enough. For example, the cosmos in

Greek science remained both limited and geocentric, in accord with the attachment of Greek total culture to the immediate, sensory, and corporeal. It was therefore difficult, according to Spengler, for the Greeks to accept an infinite universe and heliocentricity: these points of view could come to prevail only in a new and different civilization with more capacity for conceiving space as such. We enter here into a somewhat dubious area, as between whether the limiting compulsions were particularly Greek or were rather due to astronomy being still in its infancy—whether it was the basic and inherent orientation of our Western civilization, or the fact that it came two thousand years later, that had most to do with our transcending the Ptolemaic system. The doubt is not helped when we realize that on the one hand Spengler was passionately convinced that all the real cultures *must* have had different sciences as well as different philosophies and arts, and on the other that historians of science tend tacitly to assume that science is and must be one.[1]

However, there is evidence which Spengler did not know that shows a development of mathematics to have occurred in East Asia quite different from that to the West, where the influence of Greek mathematics spread to India and Islam as well as to Europe and produced systems which, while not quite uniform, were at any rate interconnected. The account comes from the profes-

[1] Hugh Miller in *History and Science* (1939) sketches a picture of the special quality of Greek mathematics which gives no evidence of influence by Spengler yet makes clear the fundamental difference of approach from modern mathematics.

sional mathematicians, Mikami and D. E. Smith, in 1912 and 1914, so that it is not open to the charge of having been warped by Spenglerian preconceptions. In brief, the story is this.

Until about A.D. 1200, Chinese mathematics was modest and hardly developed beyond arithmetical operations. During the thirteenth century, there arose in China a type of algebra of unknown origin, known as the "celestial element" method. This reached a culmination with Ch'in Chiu-shao in 1247, and Chu Shih-chieh in 1303. Its most characteristic feature is described as the use of the "monad" unity as representative of the unknown. It operated with negative as well as positive quantities, these being indicated in black and red. It is hardly conceivable that this algebra was wholly of uninfluenced native Chinese origin; but there are almost no reports of Arabic or Indic symbols or devices. This stream of algebra never formed part of the classic educational system of China; nor is there mention of its having been put to serious technological, astronomical, or practical application. It was taught, by some of those who knew it, to any who were attracted and wished to learn it for its own sake. It did not enter into the examinations for office, and was understood by few formal scholars. It rated as nonclassic and popular learning, and the official scholars often misunderstood and then forgot it. When subsequently a historic interest in it was rearoused, some of the principal books on this algebra had become lost. They were recovered only in the nineteenth century from Korean reprints.

From Korea, practice of this art or science passed to Japan, smouldered there for a time, until in early Tokugawa times, around 1600, it was revived and developed farther by a series of Japanese students, the greatest of whom, Seki Kowa, 1642–1708, was a contemporary of Newton. Successors carried on various ramifications of the method until the Meiji era, 1868, extensions of some originality continuing to be produced into the nineteenth century. Some of these Japanese mathematicians probably were of good family, but the art passed, as in China, as a sort of popular intellectual sport, which, say like chess in the West, possessed a literature and schools, and recognized masters of its own.

It is difficult to describe a strange mathematical system in words. Some indication of the aberrancy of this one from all others is given by the following points or demonstrations. It dealt with the ellipse, cycloid, catenary, and other curves, but not with the parabola or hyperbola. It investigated cylindrical but not conic sections. Inscribed squares and their derivatives were used for circle measuring, not hexagons, nor usually were any circumscribed polygons used. Some of these peculiarities do not strike very deep, but they do show independence of Western mathematics. Above all, there is in this East Asiatic algebra no sign of its being derived from geometry, nor of its being aware of any geometry. In fact, the East Asiatic civilization possessed no systematic geometry until Euclidean geometry was subsequently introduced by European missionaries.

Granted that some as yet undetermined stimulus from

the West probably started this algebra off, its development was purely Chinese and Japanese. It may, I think, fairly be considered a largely independent style of mathematics, with its own premises, manner, and problems. That it did not come to play any important part in East Asiatic culture is perhaps due to the fact that when it originated, this culture was already old and set, with a rigorously defined system of scholarship and education, and had left little if any room for a new mathematics to contribute either prestige or practical aids. The accepted style of learning in the Far East was heavily verbal and belletristic. There was also an advanced technology; but this was empirical and scarcely leaned at all on science, which remained unsystematized and random. The East Asian civilization just never did make space for any considerable pure science to grow in. Mathematics comes nearest of the sciences to being able to develop in a vacuum. The East Asian algebra soon died again through lack of cultural soil, both in China and subsequently, more slowly, in Japan; but while it lived it achieved a distinctive style of its own.

It is pertinent to add that we have come to look upon mathematics and science as universals, free from specific cultural adhesions—or, where such remain, we hold that they are only unfortunate detriments. We say that science is international, but by that we also mean intercultural. Where a population lacks science, we are wont to deny them full civilization, almost as if they were illiterate. In short, contemporary science has actually attained to the condition of complete internal interflow which

I have outlined as impending in the visual arts. We tend to forget, therefore, that in its beginnings science also varied according to population, was regional and dependent on its culture, and showed much more stylization than today, when it varies and individuates little except in time.

Witness, for the former diverse styling of science, the three separate and fitful devisings in history of systems of position numerals and signs for zero—Babylonian, Maya, and Indian—two of which had so tenuous a hold in their culture that they perished again. Or the basic difference in mathematics, astronomy, and calendar between civilizations as nearly adjacent and simultaneous as the Mesopotamian and Egyptian. Or how the Greeks turned Egyptian geometry from a method of measuring land for taxation into a pure science of their own.

Well, all this may serve to show that the course or historic behavior of the sciences is fairly close to that of the arts, and that something at least akin to style can be traced in intellectual as well as aesthetic growth.

From here we pass to our third topic: style in entire civilizations. How far is it justified, and how far profitable, to extend the concept of style to total cultures?

This might mean, first and most conservatively, an assembly of all the several styles occurring in a civilization, with due consideration of their interactions and interinfluencings.

Second, it is conceivable that these interactions produce something like a superstyle in its own right, and that this is definable or at least describable.

If there is such a super- or total-culture style, it would certainly be extremely interesting to isolate, and might be of theoretical importance.

One thing I want to establish at the outset, though I shall come back to it more at length later.

Any whole-culture style that may be discoverable must be regarded as composite in origin, secondary, and derivative. If the direction of our thought is reversed from this and the total style is posited as primary, we are inevitably deriving the well-known particular styles in the culture from a much less well-known, more unsure and vague origin or totality. The full significance which the several segmentary styles have may not be evident until all their interactions have been traced and the sum total of qualities in the culture begins to be visible. But the method of procedure must be from the particulars to the larger whole, else we lose ourselves in unprovable intuitions or even mysticism. The larger the whole, the more of a construct it necessarily is. But a construct built up from particulars, or supported step by step with particulars, has a chance of being prevailingly true—at least for its day—and significant; whereas one bold Gordian stroke is almost sure to be largely a miss. Most problem knots must be picked. Those that the sword can cut, have generally long since been severed.

An ethnologist with travel and field experience, and not too preoccupied with merely abstract or universal problems, mostly deals with small societies of a few thousand souls, whose culture is usually not too highly diversified internally but is contrastively well differentiated from other nonliterate cultures, especially those at a distance. The degree of insulation between areas is marked, affording a favorable soil both for originality and specialization of culture in separate areas and for strong co-ordination and homogeneity to develop within each little society. Further, the mass of the culture is modest, compared with that of a great civilization, so that it can without undue difficulty be mastered in its main lines and perceived with perspective, as a whole. This is one of the opportunities that the profession of ethnologist brings with it—this plus the experience of firsthand living contact with a novel way of life.

It is therefore not surprising that ethnologists, and anthropologists in general, have shown unusual propensity to transfer their approach from their little cultures to the great ones and to examine these with a strong faith that they also possess a pervasive unity and a strong internal co-ordination that can be formulated.

It is of interest that such formulations by anthropologists, alike of great civilizations or little cultures, have turned out to be couched in great measure in psychological terms. For instance, Benedict's famous *Patterns of Culture* portrays the total style of three select small cultures. The exemplifications of evidence are cultural: customs, beliefs, manners, ideals. But more and more as the portrait is developed does psychology emerge; and the final summation is in terms of temperament and even psychiatry: the Zuni are Apollonian, the Dobuans paranoid, the Kwakiutl megalomanic. Various analyses by Mead, Bateson, Gorer, and others, and Benedict's own study of Japanese culture, *The Chrysanthemum and the Sword*, trend similarly toward ethos, national temperament or disposition—character seen as a precipitate of customary behavior.

I am not sure how to construe this psychological result. It may be due to a bent in the ethnologists. Contrarily, it may lie in the nature of things. Possibly when we get away from the aesthetic or intellectual, from fashion, gastronomy, or other segments of life, and try to portray the style or quality of a whole civilization, such a generalization perhaps inevitably slips on to the psychological level. Could it be that portrayal in cultural terms necessarily remains somewhat additively descriptive, and that the effort to generalize—as in passing from a strand or segment to the whole civilization—cannot but tend to transmute the findings into psychology?

I know that I do not see clearly at this fork of the road. I once made a deliberate effort to outline the psychology of a nonliterate culture that I was familiar with—to describe the type of personality normally produced by living in the institutions, values, and ways of the culture. When I showed the portrait to psychologists, they seemed to think it contained little characterization of psychology but was still largely in cultural terms.

It looks as if we might have to admit some difference between adjacent disciplines as to territory they claim or disown.

I have also to admit that the concept of style as applicable to whole cultures is, like most extensions, somewhat less definite than its original, narrower meaning. However, the subject is still young and undeveloped, and I shall return to it.

At the moment, however, let us try to push on experimentally into a still further extension. I want to test what happens when we try to follow the idea of style on to the frankly organic level. The term organic here is not a metaphor; I mean by it: biological. I have briefly ventured this suggestion once or twice before, in print, but without eliciting a reaction.

While my remarks on this head are not merely metaphorical, I realize that they are analogical. Style in organic life cannot be identical with style in art and culture. The word life as such of course refers to a different category of phenomena from culture; or where the two sets of phenomena occur associated or intertwined, as in man, they possess quite distinct aspects.

Briefly, life is a reproductive continuum which is extremely conservative. In its higher manifestations it succeeds in achieving a marked degree of individuation, combined with remarkable faculties, including considerable initiative. Such individuation and faculties seem somehow incompatible, in the nature of the world, with an unvarying continuity. At any rate they are expressed in largely disparate organic bodies, or "individuals." The connections between these individuals, while maintaining a true continuity—that of heredity—are exceedingly compressed, so that the flow of life seems, to unanalytic eyes, a repetitive succession of like bodies. The mechanism of this process of course is organic heredity or genetics, about which an enormous amount of knowledge has been accumulated in the past fifty years.

We have in short in the higher forms of life—if I may for a moment rephrase some trite obviousnesses for my special purposes—we have continuity residing in the species, which normally is highly conservative and slow-changing, but which consists of individuals that are as largely separate as it is possible for them to be, yet, on account of the continuity, are also essentially repetitive of one another. It is really a unique situation in nature. We are wont to take this uniqueness for granted because, phenomenally, it is so familiar.

In man, who alone has culture, the same species-individual relation and hereditary mechanism are of course present, but they have become much less relevant, because of a new factor, consisting of the products, tangible and intangible, of individuals living in groups. These products are what we call culture. They maintain an existence of their own, which is associated with the groups of individuals, in fact is dependent on them; and yet the products have also a certain independence, in that they largely affect and modify one another. This inter-influencing of the cultural products is normally much greater than the influence which human individuals as individuals, as hereditarily constituted members of the species, have on the products. The cultural products, not bound by heredity, are far more plastic than the individuals; they vary in larger arcs. This in turn enables them to influence other culture in the direction of increased change; and so onward. The result is that while culture as well as life has continuity, it shows, within the limits set by life, far greater and more rapid variability. Its reoccurrences and continuations are much less repetitive than are the individuals in an organic species.

On account of this difference in variability, culture appears to us a far more natural and fit medium than life for style to grow in. There seems an infinity of room in culture for an infinity of styles to develop. The inherent plasticity of culture probably also contributes to the generally rapid flow of the course of style. The congruence or consistency which marks cultural style is relatively readily achieved on account of its plasticity and lability; but also readily exhausted, and reachieved, or partly achieved or modified.

By contrast, that which we may call "style" or its counterpart in living organisms, and which resides in the organisms themselves, has been painfully acquired by aeons of selection and is maintained with great tenacity by heredity. Because of the slowness and difficulty with which consistency of organic "style" has been acquired, the consistency or congruence is likely to be much firmer. The species may perish, but its "style" will not be modified lightly while it survives, compared with cultural style.

Perhaps I have been talking in seeming parables, or

dressing old tritenesses up in fancy words. Let me try to restate my point more concretely.

I would suggest as the closest organic parallel to style in culture the over-all quality of consistent form of well-characterized organisms; that quality of form, especially, which is basic to a definitely characteristic functioning of the animal or plant; that which gives it typical powers or habitus or temperament or ethos. An example would be the formal qualities which differentiate greyhound and bulldog; or those which express the streamlining of fish, or of birds. These are qualities visible in form (and even measurable there, if one so wishes), inhering in structure and in functioning; usually widely pervasive in the structure and hence affecting many organs; therefore giving a real coherence and congruence of form-quality to most of the organs or parts. This coherence is what organisms share with style in culture.

In a bird, for instance, the flowing contours of the body, the smooth covering of overlapping feathers, the pointed head, the retractile legs, the absence of external ears or other appendages, the hollow bones, all contribute to the successful functioning of flight. Even more remote characteristics prove to be associated: the high body temperature along with the warmth of feathers minimizes the loss of heat in rapid motion through the air; the dominance of the eyes among the sense organs contributes to successful search, steering, and landing; the rapid growth of the young shortens their danger period of preflight defenselessness.

A similar consistency of plan and function, of co-ordination of parts in a given direction to a well-characterized, consistent ethos, is evident in the falcon and in the tiger, the octopus and the ant, the cactus and the oak.

Here perhaps is something more than a metaphor, a genuine and significant organic analogy to the distinctive but pervading physiognomic qualities possessed by styles, possibly including whole-culture styles. In a culture, the parts of the style are mainly not in a relation of vital, indispensable interdependence, such as that of organs in a living body whose functional interdependence is of the strictest and tightest kind. In a culture the parts tend to exist in a relation of assimilation of form and quality to one another, and to the form and quality of the whole. This coherence of assimilated form and quality in culture corresponds to coherence of inherited structural organization, to habitus, temperament, disposition on the organic or psychological level. It is in fact expressible, to a certain extent, in outright psychological terms.

There are three specific respects in which the organic analogy to style seems to hold, as here redefined. First, a species, or for that matter a genus or even an order or phylum, has a history. It represents an achieved evolution, which is unique, not repetitive in itself. This is true also of culture. Both a species and a culture or style have evolved through responses to their total and flucutating past environments, plus internal changes—mutational innovations and inventive or creative innovations respectively.

Second, just as a species consists of a stream of essentially repetitive individual organisms, so the society through which alone a culture can exist is a stream of human individuals down the generations. The species or genus is a form common to the individuals who constitute its material substance: a culture or civilization is the form taken by the products of a society within the human species.

Third, every species is full of adaptations, often recognizable in a marvelous measure: but we know almost nothing of the causality by which these adaptive marvels of form and function were produced. They would be much easier to explain in a teleological world view, if we allowed design, wisdom, purpose, or final causes in the universe, as we cannot allow them as scientific positivists. So we assume there was efficient causality at work in producing the adaptations: the myriad unknown specific causes are blanketed under some process like natural selection. Yet it is important to remember that in the great majority of cases we do not know the specific causes of the particular features of an organic species. We do not know specifically what caused the fang and claw and sinew and eye and lashing tail to conform in that one fearful symmetry. This near ignorance is strictly paralleled in regard to civilizations: we know as good as nothing of what produced their wholes. And as little can we mostly say what specifically made the specific parts cohere as they do in a style. In both cases, the conformity and consistency of form makes styles as acceptable as

*79*

species, and endows them with significance even though we possess only imperfect knowledge of what made them.

While we are navigating in this somewhat misty realm of similarities maintained in spite of fundamental distinctness, let me outline one more idea. This is in the realm of philosophy of science, and how its methods seem to be influenced by our natures.

I start from the assumption that what we have most immediate consciousness and knowledge of is ourselves, our own bodies and feelings. From this subjective core, in the life history of each of us and in the history of early human knowledge, understanding slowly spreads out. The farther out it spreads as something systematized, the easier and more productive does understanding become. Those parts of nature which lie farthest from ourselves are the easiest for science to explore: lifeless matter and the cosmos. Physics and astronomy are the earliest substantive sciences. Anthropomorphism is most easily shaken off there, and a new order of objectivity is most readily revealed. Chemistry lags somewhat, perhaps partly because it deals with qualities rather than shapes, but probably also because it is from chemistry that the main bridge proves to lead through biochemistry and physiology between the inorganic realm and ourselves as organisms. Understanding of organisms, especially in their aspects as whole individuals, when they most resemble ourselves, has been still slower and more difficult for our race to acquire. We are aware of their enormous complexities and variabilities; experimentation, that invaluable tool, has been difficult to apply, as the brevity of the history of vital experiment in genetics shows. In short, the nearer we come to the subject matter—namely, ourselves—which is most immediate in our consciousness, and which we might therefore expect to be the most complacent to methodical scientific approach, the more resistive does it show itself. I suspect that it is psychology, the methodical study of ourselves, which is inherently the most difficult science. Particularly does that seem to be so when psychology is holistic, interested in the entire person: if we break off a bit of it, such as the faculty of learning, scientific method is not too difficult to apply for a little way. However, even then the native resistance of the material is evident in a certain slenderness of result: the ore of psychology does seem low grade compared with that of other sciences, no matter how technically skillful the attack upon it.

When we progress beyond psychology in the opposite direction, into kinds of phenomena that overlie and presuppose psychological activity—can in part be reduced to it, much as psychology in its turn is partly reducible to physiology and chemistry—I venture to suggest that on this opposite side the same situation holds, and results in a paradox: that the scientific study of society and especially of culture is inherently less difficult and more readily productive of understanding than the scientific study of persons. Certainly the greater co-ordinations and configurations are more easily recognized; the scale is larger, perspectives appear, and a historical approach is feasible. I venture to say that we already possess as much generalized understanding of cultural style, because it is historic, as of personal or individual style, though that has been recognized much longer.

At any rate, I submit the suggestion. If it fails to convince, it may at least serve to explain somewhat the idiosyncrasy or temerity of trying to explore the dim, outermost bounds.

# 4

# Spengler

OF ALL who have dealt comparatively with civilization, Oswald Spengler should in certain ways be nearest
to the heart of a cultural anthropologist, such as I am. He
is comparative in the broadest sense. He is wholly non-
ethnocentric and a complete cultural relativist. He is
concerned with understanding culture autonomously, in
its own terms. He does not derive it from biological constitution or heredity, nor from geography and natural
environment, nor does he try to reduce it to physiology
or biochemistry. His contrastive interests are strong, his
powers of characterization marked, protecting him

against taking refuge in superficial uniformities or vague commonplaces.

These are qualities toward which my own personality leans. Spengler therefore affected me strongly when I first came to know his *Decline of the West*. If I had been able to embrace his views, I should no doubt have done so with enthusiasm. Instead, analysis of his work cumulatively revealed constant needless exaggerations, dogmatism, vehemence of conviction, blind spots, inability to balance evidence. By now, after nearly forty years, his defects as scholar or scientist are generally recognized. Sorokin treats him almost too considerately in the chapter he accords him in his *Social Philosophies* of 1950; and H. Stuart Hughes two years later in his *Oswald Spengler: A Critical Estimate*—the soundest book on the man —tempers his rejection both of Spengler's doctrine and his method with recognition of his imaginative talent and intellectual importance. As the years pass, I incline more and more to see Germanic "expressionism"—overexpression, most the rest of the world would call it—as Spengler's cardinal vice, which he shared with Nietzsche as with Wagner and with Hitler and with thousands of lesser thinkers, writers, painters, and others. It is essentially an unmeasuredness, at once a symptom and a further feed-back cause of Germany's never having shared quite fully on terms of equality in Western civilization except transiently in the interval of Kant, Goethe, and Beethoven. It is a Titanic temperament, but in its extravagance and extremity, it verges toward the pathological.

I too have taken Spengler apart in my 1944 *Configura-*

*tions of Culture Growth,* and have there specified my disagreements. Instead of piling up further negative criticism, I will therefore proceed to state what I consider the legitimate problem that Spengler has put on the docket of history and scientific research, and how far and in what sense the problem can be answered.

This problem as I see it concerns the degree of coherence and congruity existing between the many parts, organs, pieces, or items of which every culture consists. Spengler himself has an answer. For each of his great cultures in their active phase, which is all that he will consent to deal with, he affirms the coherence to be total. One quality pervades the whole of each of them for its duration, he says. He not only reduces each culture to its prime symbol, but derives it from that symbol, whose expression it is. Thus, a confined one-directional way is the symbol for ancient Egypt, but the indeterminate wandering way for China; the congregation in the cavern, or eternally vaulted space, symbolizes the Magian culture, but the present, sensory, individual corporeal body, Classic Antiquity; pure and limitless space is the symbol of the West, but the plane without end for the as yet unborn Russian culture. It is evident that these are pregnant poetic images. But the mere fact that they might have been coined by a Blake or a Melville renders it unlikely that they will serve as useful tools for a nonrhapsodical interpretation of history.

There is also the difficulty that vast quantities of cultural material—inventions, religions, alphabets, and what not—are shared between various cultural entities, are known to have passed from one civilization to another. Spengler meets the point with typical offhand insolence. He denies that there has been much such diffusion or intercultural transmission of consequence: it cannot really happen, except as nonsignificant accident; true cultures are impervious to each other, he insists. When they do borrow, they make over their borrowings in their own manner, congruent with themselves. This would mean that what is significant in the Greeks having learned their letters from the Phoenicians, the Romans from the Greeks, and we (through our ancestors) from the Romans, was not in each case the fact that a nonliterate people became literate, but that they altered the writing which they borrowed into a stylistically new form of script. Greek letters were changed in shape, order, or denotation from Phoenician, Roman from the Greek, and our modern ones at least in details from the Roman. In short, it is the visible *style* of writing the letters that is significant to Spengler, not the enormous effect and influence which ability to read and write has on the life of a society that has previously done without. The latter phenomenon, with all its massivity, leaves him cold: it is a happening that can recur in any situation, or in several cultures; but the style of a script is distinctive; and distinctive differentials being what attract and interest him, he blandly pushes the rest aside as of no moment.

Why has such a differentiated style, however minute, significance? Because, he says, all the styles of a culture—of script, representation, decoration, sculpture, poetry, music, philosophy, science, politics—are congruent in having a common quality, which is the expression of the culture as an entity. This is what Spengler declares dogmatically: he cannot prove it, because he assumes it to begin with. *A prioris* are notoriously hard to prove, except by selected evidence.

However, there is a possibility here. Cultural qualities ought expectably to be more alike among the traits actually associated in a given culture than in a random selection from several cultures. We can discard Spengler's fiat that materials from one culture *must* be alike in quality, and that *all* of it must be alike because it is all the expression of one symbol representing one soul. But it is not necessary to discard his *all* for a *none*—to assume that because much material drifts fortuitously between civilizations, it must all be drifting, and that normally none of it has originated in the culture in which we find it. No one, to my knowledge, has ever outrightly affirmed so nihilistic a doctrine. Franz Boas, with his critical negativism toward all anthropological schemes about culture, may perhaps at times have seemed to be close to such a view, because he liked to keep all intellectual doors open to any and every possibility. But he was much too exact and sound ever to commit himself to so universal a negation. Robert Lowie's "shreds and patches theory"—which was not really a theory but a passing allusion—is an allusion to the history, to the original sources, of the materials composing a culture, not to their ultimate structuring.

In other words, it is only sense to expect that Spengler's assertion that everything in a culture must be equally tinctured with one quality characteristic of the culture is untrue because it is an oversimple absolute. The claim probably is the wish-fulfillment of the way Spengler would have liked the world to be. But, contrariwise, it is only sense to realize that a flat denial of any and all stylistic congruence within a culture would be as extreme an absolute as Spengler's total affirmation. The truth evidently lies between; and the problem is: Where does it lie? This is presumably a problem that can be solved, albeit no doubt only very gradually, by evidence and unbiased analysis. And it is a large problem of great interest. It was Spengler who, while taking his point of view from Nietzsche, who had said: "Culture is unity of artistic style in all the life manifestations of a people" [1]— it was Spengler who thrust the problem into wider consideration, even though, as he was evoking it, he simultaneously moved to kill the problem off by dogmatically affirming its final answer.

Let us try to sharpen the formulation of this question of how far a culture may legitimately and profitably be viewed as a sort of style, perhaps something like what I have already called a superstyle, or a style of styles: a total style of life.

To get off the level of abstract argument, I would like to examine concrete examples. It will be convenient, as well as fair to Spengler, to take the two of his examples on

[1] Nietzsche, *Geburt der Tragoedie*, in *Ges. Werke* (1924), I, 183.

which he has most to say, the ancient Classic culture and the mediaeval-modern Western.[2] I will first summarize the evidence he alleges as showing common quality or ethos in each of these cultures, and then inquire, not whether he is right or wrong, but how much he may be right, and especially by what process the common quality or superstyle may have been developed.

I shall now try to summarize Spengler's portrayal of the Classical culture as a style.

This is the Graeco-Roman civilization, largely Hellenic but completed by Rome, and called simply Hellenic by Toynbee. Its period according to Spengler is 1100 B.C. to A.D. 200. It had a formative or precultural stage from 1600 to 1100; this was Mycenaean and late Minoan.

This Classical culture is that of Nietzsche's Apollinian man, who aims at measure, limitation, tangibility, time-lessness. It is concerned with bodily reality, sensory form, the moment, stasis, boundary. It does not face extension, passage of time, past or future, energy, conflict. Exemplifications of this culture are:

The polis is the wall-enclosed city which is also an autonomous state; all its citizens can and do assemble

---

[2] More of his argument concerns these two cultures than all the others together. There is a fair body of data and discussion on Magian-Arabic, but astonishingly little in the way of cited phenomena on Egypt, Mesopotamia, India, and China. This means that Spengler's thinking was comparative in intent rather than in execution, and that he might and did have strong convictions on surprisingly scattered concrete knowledge. I have added an appendix setting forth this disproportion.

within earshot. An empire—Athenian, Spartan, Roman —consists of other city-states, or barbarian tribes, conquered by one city-state.

Wealth, other than land, takes the form of money, coined metal—round, compact, hard, transportable. This was the invention of Hellenized Lydians and was given its spread and its most beautiful forms by Greeks. Next to metal, movable wealth consisted increasingly of enslaved human bodies.

In art, the single, free-standing, compact, usually nude statue was dominant over groups, reliefs, and painting.

In architecture, sober, simple structures of limited size and aspiration were characteristic.

Music followed only the melodic line: instruments— such as flute and lyre—were simple, few-noted or monotone, and not used together or only in the smallest groupings.

In drama, the limitations or negations of the "three unities" are significant; also the depersonalizing masks and impersonal chorus.

The typical Greek mathematics was geometry, which was visualizable and constructible, corporeally limited and measurable, whether plane or solid. Its farthest development into "conic sections" still shows these qualities. Algebra with its fluid emphasis on relations was lacking—Spengler considers the Diophantine algebra non-Greek, Magian in origin. Greek arithmetic dealt primarily with integral numbers and their theory. The only powers were the second and third, and these were conceived as the square and the cube of physical corporeality. Greek mathematics lacked the concepts of irrational numbers, negative quantities, indefinite or algebraic numbers, zero or infinity as quantities, function.

Physics was mainly static and evaded the time factor. Astronomy conceived a solidly contained, limited universe, bounded by the adamant sphere of the fixed stars. Extension is not space in our sense, but corporeality: "nature abhors a vacuum," was the ancient view.

The history of Classic antiquity was essentially contemporaneous, written in large part by participants, such as Thucydides, Polybius, Caesar. Its span was short; it lacked time depth. The Greeks were weak in chronology, short in memory and records as compared with Egyptians, Mesopotamians, Chinese; unimaginative as to change, without care for tomorrow.

Religion consisted of cults indissolubly attached to spots, with little feeling other than of such attachment, but a mythology of sensuous form, from Olympian gods to nymphs and fauns, which was and became increasingly basic to aesthetic activity rather than to belief and action.

I now summarize Spengler's view of Western culture as a style.—European or Occidental culture took shape about A.D. 900, or perhaps during the tenth century, with the emergence to consciousness of European nationalities. Its precultural stage lasted from 500 to 900, thus comprising the Dark Age and the Carolingian period. The "civilizational" phase of the culture—in Spengler's hostile sense of the word—is now upon us—since about

1800—and is likely to last till 2200 or beyond, on the basis of his parallelism of courses.

This is the culture of Faustian man with his aspiration and restless striving. It is directed toward interest in time, distance, infinity, energy, struggle, tension, the dynamic, the boundless, and ultimate.

Politically, its vehicle is the national state instead of the city-state, with a dynasty giving the desired continuity. Towns are only estates within the state.

Economic relations revolve about credit and double-entry bookkeeping. Coined money has become a meaningless anachronism of the heritage from Classic culture.

In art, first painting and later music dominate over corporeal sculpture. In painting, successive stages are marked by perspective, with its vanishing point; chiaroscuro, the broken line; impressionism and representation of atmosphere. In music, melody becomes multiple in counterpoint, and then harmonic. The orchestra develops, also polyphonic instruments: the organ and then the piano.

In architecture, Gothic cathedrals contrast with Greek temples in their aspiration and in seeking instead of avoiding ambitious structural problems; also in their deliberate multiplications and elaborations.

In mathematics, the calculus of fluxions or infinitesimals, analytic geometry (the conversion of geometry into algebra), the concepts of function and limit, plus all the now used apparatus which was avoided by the Greeks, are typical.

Physics first became dynamic instead of static with its

consideration of the rate of falling bodies, and proceeded to deal increasingly with time as a factor.

Astronomy first turned from being pivoted here and now to heliocentrism, then went on to the concept of an unlimited universe. Space became extension instead of bodily size.

A genuine history in depth arose; the world could now be conceived as history.

It was Occidental culture, still in its Gothic phase, that first devised mechanical clocks for continuous record of time. Characteristic too are the inventions which conquered distance: firearms, railroads, telephones, many others. Printing served unlimited multiplication.

Occidental religion is not made very clear by Spengler. Sometimes he seems to feel its religion to be a Christianized Germanic epic;[3] genuine Christianity he appears to consider to have been limited to early Christianity, and to reserve to the Magian culture. But there is in the West a strong sense of tragic fate, as in the Eddic Völuspa and the Götterdämmerung.

The foregoing are Spengler's two fullest physiognomic characterizations, summarized briefly, and free of his divagations and undisciplined associations.[4]

It is in the contrast of these two cultures that there resides the core of whatever specific value Spengler's

[3] *The Decline of the West*, trans. Atkinson (1926–1928), I, 399–401.

[4] Incidentally, much of the essence of this contrast of the two civilizations was first expressed, in poetic form, by Goethe in the long second act in the Second Part of *Faust*, in which Faust and Mephistopheles visit the world of classical mythology.

work may have. These two cultures he knows and experiences as he knows and feels no others. It seems likely that he actually began his thinking with a balancing comparison of them, and then extended it to other cultures. At any rate, the crux of his method is deployed on these two. If his formulations on the Classic and the Occidental civilization fail, all his others, which are so much less substantiated, fail even more. What he says about these two is the citadel of his thought.

What then is the essential nature of Spengler's promulgation? He himself speaks of a physiognomy, sometimes of a style. I would call it an endeavor to express the style of a culture. It is characterization of pervasive form, of Gestalt in modern parlance; total form seen not item by item but as a whole, arrived at as an intellectual unit as if it were a foundry casting. It is an interweaving of patterns related in their similarity, in their copresence within the culture, and in their cofunctioning toward a common larger quality in the whole culture. It is this, translated into sober English, which it seems to me Spengler is trying to express. How successful he is, how real his tyings together are, is the problem before us.

The Greek walled city dominating its tiny autonomous state, the small disk of minted metal, the solitary statue of human corporeality, the soberly restricted temple, the single-line, small-compass melody, the drama within the unities, the visualizable, carvable mathematics, the static physics, the universe confined in its adamant sphere—are these characteristic Classic culture phenomena really alike in quality? Or is the likeness merely metaphorical? Are these cultural creations at all inter-related like the coadapted organs in one body, or like the expressions of one major purpose, the multiform reactions of a single temperament?

The same question holds of course for our Western civilization. Are we really to unite, into a larger whole that possesses some quality analogous to organic unity, as Spengler at times said—a quality more or less like expressions in a single style, I would say—is it legitimate to relate the Gothic cathedral; painting that uses perspective, shadows, and atmosphere; polyphonic harmony in music; double-entry bookkeeping; the mathematics of calculus, function, and limits; dynamic physics and astronomy of infinite space, clocks and sense of historic depth—do these all share some qualities of a style?

If there is some significant similarity in these products of one civilization, then there is something usable that can be salvaged from Spengler in spite of all his emotionality, dogmatism, and excess. But if we deny reality to a seeming common stylistic quality running through the particular items here listed, then there appears to be little left in the Spengler approach.

The answer depends on one's presuppositions. A causal explanation of historic connections to account for similarities is ruled out. One cannot seriously advance an argument that, following the sequence of their appearance, Gothic architecture caused the invention of clocks; that these clocks caused the discovery of perspective in painting and the devising of musical harmony; that these two activities in turn had a hand in producing

Copernican astronomy and analytic geometry, and so on. Nor is the case really better if instead of seeing $A$ as causing $B$, and $B$, $C$, one falls back on a primal $X$ which causes $A$ and $B$ and $C$ alike. Such an underlying $X$ is too general and vague to be convincing—too much like Spengler's prime symbol. Indeed such an $X$ is likely to be only a redescription of the historic trend of events, verbally cloaked as a cause.

The only way we could expect a causal chain reaction of fixed order $A, B, C, D$ . . . $N$ to happen is in an isolated, closed-off, self-sufficient situation. That kind of situation is easy to devise in an experimental setup—in fact it is just what laboratory experiment consists of. But that sort of a precisely determining situation does not normally get carried out with much success in the large world of nature—with one notable exception: the repetition of biological individuals within their species. When the egg is fertilized it may get smashed or the chick get eaten or the bird stay ill-fed and die young: but it is predetermined that it will come out a hen and not an eagle or squirrel or basilisk. This is, however, an affair of repetitive individuals within the genetic continuum of a species; and each individual is about as nearly isolated as possible—in all higher animals—and as nearly self-sufficient as occurs in natural phenomena on this our planet.

But the history of man and his culture is not at all a straightly channeled continuum like what used to be called germ plasm and is now construed as the genes in their chromosomes. Instead, it is an indefinitely branching, meandering, widening, anastomizing, reuniting, crossing and recrossing flow. Nor are successive civilizations at all like hens or eagles in their recurrent likeness. Least of all like them, in fact, would be Spengler's monadal cultures, each of which he sees as wholly distinct and qualitatively different from all others, so as to be only faintly intelligible to members of other cultures.

In fact, the actual parallel to Spengler's view of culture would be a biological world in which a hen, an eagle, a squirrel, and a basilisk, plus one individual each of perhaps a half-dozen other species, would come into being without ancestors, would live through parallel stages and for about the same duration, and would then atrophy into a skin-covered skeleton or hollow shell, leaving no sucessors or posterity. And all this without connections or interrelations between the monadal exemplars—each perpetually turned inward to live out its inherent destiny.

This is the fantastic projection that could be made of Spengler's doctrine back on to the biological world of reality. I cite it especially in order to refute a mistaken view which attempts to dispose of Spengler as having attempted to understand culture by organic analogy. This is one thing I am confident Spengler did *not* do, because he did not really think in biological terms. He seems to me to have been singularly uninterested in biological phenomena or the history of life except as expressed in human culture—and only certain manifestations of that.

He did use the term "organic" metaphorically, for

relationships or associations that were inherent, strong, and enduring. It is a natural term for a historian, philosopher, or man of letters so to use. It is not a term which a natural scientist would use except with intended specific biological significance. With Spengler the word is probably a heritage of eighteenth-century usage, when the contrast of organic with inorganic or mechanical took on a new verve, perhaps especially so in Germany.

For instance, Adelung, in his 1782 *Geschichte der Cultur*, outlines a history of the human species in eight stages, each comparable to a stage of ontogenetic development, that is, of individual maturation. Thus the third stage, from Moses to 683 B.C., is designated as "The Human Race as a Boy" and the eighth and last, from A.D. 1520 on, as "Man in Enjoyment of His Full Enlightenment" (*Der Mensch im Aufgeklaerten Genusse*). This was a real attempt to lean on the biological parallel. Spengler inherited fragments of the terminology, but did not lean on biology.

True, Spengler does see "growth" in his cultures; but who does not? Toynbee uses the word, Danilevsky also, I have used it. Also, Spengler saw the growth as irreversible—a phenomenon most familiar to us from organic life. Possibly that familiarity helped emphasize his feeling for cultural death as the counterpart of biological death. But when he finally summarizes the corresponding courses of his cultures, in tabulations more orderly and systematized than anything else he presented, he uses the seasons, not phases of life, as connotive headings for the stages of the cultural course. No one would therefore accuse him of believing that human culture was based on climate or astronomy.

It is further true that spring and summer and winter suggest the growth and decay of plant life, and that Spengler was undoubtedly aware of the metaphor. While we are all in agreement that definable terms carry us farther into exact understanding than do metaphors and analogies, yet when the processes dealt with are not yet precisely conceived because not precisely known, one has to use the best adumbrative terms available. It seems to me clear from the whole tenor of his *Untergang* that Spengler's view of culture was not infected by organicism—say, as the racists were—but that he tried desperately to see culture in autonomous terms, in full self-sufficiency. If anything, he went too far in this direction: he left culture so wholly isolated in the cosmos that in effect he reified it into an unexplained essence or series of unexplained entities.

I conclude then that Spengler in his thinking was the reverse of an organicist, though he did use biological terms metaphorically in default of available cultural ones. He also did not organize his data in accord with cause, or even generally in order of sequence. His three chronological tables are a concession and a mistake, as Hughes observes. They are rigid; their gaps and ambiguities stand up naked; they have lost "the imaginative imprecision" of his historical perspective.

What is it that one can do in dealing intellectually with a physiognomy or style?

First, of course, a physiognomy must be perceived.

The practicing or creative visual artist goes on from there to kinaesthetic response activity; the scholar to intellectual apprehension, synthetic rather than analytic, and charged perhaps with feeling almost as much as the artist's. But expression in words of what is apprehended encounters resistance. Barriers to communication pile up, such as the artist does not have to wrestle with. The expounder of a style is driven toward a private or elect language and metaphor, to using words with special connotive meaning.

If this is true in verbal portrayal of a poetic, pictorial, or musical style, the difficulties should be greater yet in conveyance of the style of a total culture. After all, the qualities of a style are concrete; in communication they must be somehow generalized, and generalization becomes harder as the scope of the style becomes greater. One means is the conscious symbol; and metaphor becomes perhaps inevitable. The strength of prime symbols for whole cultures, like the "vaulted cavern" or "unending plane," is proportional to the number and vigor of allusive threads that run out from them into the huge mass of phenomena referred to.

At that, however, no phrase-length symbol can represent very much of so large a thing as a civilization is. Recital of traits or characteristics cannot be dispensed with. But how keep this from being merely enumerative? How organize and concentrate it?

The available method is the co-ordination of concrete phenomena that agree in sharing a quality, and going on from that to overco-ordinations. In the case of a particular art style, the scope of the things co-ordinated is not too broad. In the case of a whole culture seen as a style, the contained phenomena are more numerous and highly diverse, and the superco-ordinations called for will be larger; but they must retain a degree of the concreteness of the original phenomena.

This, I would say, is what Spengler has to a large extent done, although mostly in a passionate and tumultuous way; he has associated parts of a culture, whose substance and immediate function are highly diverse, but which nevertheless do carry a common quality.

There *is* something common to vertical cathedrals and perspective in painting and musical counterpoint and musical harmony—an intrinsic set of qualities which they share—call them interrelations of distance and of the multiple. And the validity of the connection is strengthened by the fact that in all other cultures but that of the West these stylistic qualities are much more faintly developed, and in part lacking.

Another step, and we can ally to these qualities of relations of space and multiplicity in Western civilization certain nonaesthetic features such as clocks, double-entry accounting, analytic geometry and calculus, and heliocentric astronomy, which manifest also the qualities of extension of time, flow, gradualism, balance, and relativism. Through these in turn, still wider areas of activity are entered and related, such as machine use, credit, communications, dynamic science, and long-range history both of man and nature. This last group of culture traits specially characterize the recent phase of our civilization, but yet root in its past.

Therewith, something of a coherent characterization of our civilization seems to be achieved. In itself, such a characterization is of course in no sense an explanation—though it would not deny causal explanation as ultimately possible. Instead, it has significance—an apprehended meaning. While such a characterization is not a hypothesis submitted for verification or disproof, there nevertheless are better and worse characterizations; more or less broad, congruent, and compelling characterizations.

In this way, then, it seems to me, cathedrals and counterpoint, clocks and calculus and credit can be construed as coexisting in relationship within one civilization, as more than disparate accidents, with a coherence through pervasive quality. And in a different civilization, such as the Classic, architecture, sculpture, drama, mathematics, science, politics, and wealth may be seen as sharing a different set of qualities—simplicity of structure, corporeal and temporal limitation, primacy of sensory form, and concentration.

How far can such a styling of a civilization go? That it can affect the entire cultural content would be an excessive claim, though Spengler at times makes the claim. After all, every society exists in a conditioning environment, and its members have basic physiological necessities to satisfy. It is only after this that free stylization of the culture can begin. Spengler was impatient of those commonplace universals which in themselves contribute nothing to a culture's physiognomy and can to a degree block or blur its characterization. So he ignored them and proceeded as if style had full autonomy in the eight cultures which in his mind did achieve a style. We do not have to grant this exorbitancy; but also we do not therefore have to deny whole-culture stylistic congruence altogether.

Another matter about which it is desirable to take a moderate position is the question of how, in general, such cultural style as there is comes to be. The simplest answer is Spengler's, to derive it all from the prime symbol; but this is also an extreme answer. Moreover, it derives the known from the less known. This less known, the underlying or prime symbol, is in fact an ex post facto construct rather than a *primum mobile;* to work from it comes near to making cause teleological. Spengler does not quite do this; for himself, he prefers to leave cause out altogether and talk of fate. But this causes him to leave the origin of his cultures and their styles floating free and unaccounted for.

My own reactions to this problem of how culture styles come to be are three, and those related. First, I should expect the congruent styling of cultures to be only partial; second, variable; and third, to take place gradually, with coherence not a mere unfolding from within but achieved increasingly by creative effort.

Any style of a whole culture would necessarily be incomplete. Not only are there always the environment and the human needs already referred to, but there are normally many interferences, such as impingements from other cultures. These may be so strong as to wreck neighbors as well as competitors; as when an advanced, wealthy, and powerful society comes into contact with a backward one. Spengler himself points out how native American culture was wiped out as an autonomous structure by a mere handful of adventurers from only the Spanish national segment of Western culture—and wiped out as it were for sport, plus some private greeds, he says with insight. Lesser intercultural impacts would have lesser effects; but except for rare situations at rare intervals there are always some impacts.

And impacts certainly vary. The receiving society can become the giver tomorrow. Its culture can contain at one and the same time foreign elements, accepted so long ago that they have become completely assimilated, and others still being resisted or modified, apart from those that never gained admittance.

I would, however, put most emphasis on the gradualness with which a society achieves a style for its culture, particularly if the society and culture are large. Just because much of the content of any culture has normally entered it from outside, time is necessary for its assimilation; and ordinarily it would enter into active congruence with the establishing or already operative style later still.

The period of emergence, growth, and formation of a distinctive culture, the duration of its creativity, and the time over which its characteristic style develops—these are closely interrelated. In fact the three activities, culture growth, creativity, and style development, may be looked upon as three aspects of one larger process. The production of new culture content, the assimilation of content from without, the forging of characteristic styles, the growth of congruence between the several contents and patterns—all this together is what constitutes the achievement of the total style of the culture. If the achievement is at all massive and notable, it requires time; although as after a while it comes into full flow, the development may be impressively rapid until the culture's apogee is reached; even then it may proceed some distance on momentum. Once the rates of growth and style formation diminish, they tend to decrease progressively, at least for a while; after which there may be a reconstitution of the culture on a restored or enlarged basis—in the latter case of course with a somewhat altered total style or physiognomy. Or, atrophy may continue, with degeneration of stylistic quality. Sometimes, the end may come through supersedence by another culture, or gradual absorption in it.

I give Spengler credit for sensing to an extraordinary degree the ideal potentialities of culture styles—even of imaginary cultures like the Magian. I think he must sometimes have seen more style in the cultures than was actually realized by their societies. So, when a culture finally reached a point where the discrepancy between its ideal style and its actuality could no longer be denied, Spengler simply repudiated the culture, began to talk of Caesarism, megalopolis, and fellaheen life-in-death, and virtually ruled the remainder of the culture out of history and out of existence.

Whole-cultural style as a coherence of pervasive qualities, then, is never total, never suddenly arrived at. It is never primary or unitary, always achieved and cumulative—like the ethos of a society or character in a person. It seems formulable, though hard to formulate. If it is elusive, it is also of notable and continued interest. In regard to our own civilization, I have deliberately used Spengler's alliterative example of cathedrals and counterpoint, calculus, credit, and clocks as a mnemonic shock device to focus attention on the problem of how far cultural items so disparate as these seem to be, may nevertheless be qualitatively interconnected as expressions of the total style of the culture.

That the members of our civilization and of others are very little aware of total style need not discourage us much. Every human language has such a patterned style —we call it its grammar—of which the speakers are unaware while speaking, but which can be discovered by analysis and can be formulated. The coherence of a grammar is never total or ideal, but is always considerable; it certainly much exceeds a catalogue of random items. Cultures are larger, more varied and complicated sets of phenomena than languages, as well as more substantive and less autonomous. But the two are interrelated —in fact, language is obviously a part of culture, and probably its precondition. So the structure of cultures, like that of languages, also seems potentially describable in terms of an over-all patterning.

Most of the working out of this problem on the totality of a civilization lies in the future; and I shall not see its outcome. After all, it is only recently that we have begun to think at all of specific civilizations as characterizable totalities. Possibly the problem of civilizations as an extension of the phenomenon of style, as Spengler so passionately adumbrated it and as I see it, is faulty in its formulation or setup. In that case, the future will recast the problem—perhaps displace it by one more germane to the phenomena and therefore more productive. In either event, I have faith that a greatly enlarged understanding of civilizations as macrophenomena is attainable, and that it will include comprehension of the part played in their constitution by style.

# 5

# Predecessors and Successors

UNDER the blanket title of "Predecessors and Successors"—to Spengler—I shall consider various scholars who have been interested in the comparison of civilizations, excepting only those whose approach has been primarily from the side of art, whom I reserve for the next chapter.

Of the predecessors, none is intrinsically very important today other than so far as he historically exemplifies some particular current of thought. I would except only the Russian Danilevsky, because he definitely represents the natural science approach; though my frame of reference will prevent my doing him full justice. Of successors, Toynbee's work stands out as emanating from history, and for the moral effect it has had; and there have begun to be a few further recruits from history. Sorokin, coming from sociology, uses historical data voluminously, but represents a systematizing approach, with the result that his dress is more different from others than his substance.

A few words, first of all, about philosophies of history —which I should perhaps have voiced before this. After this page, I shall not concern myself further with them. The term is Voltaire's, and he wrote the first one. It is essentially a general or universal history from the point of view of eighteenth-century rational enlightenment. It is mainly in narrative form, with the philosophizing incidental.

Herder a few decades later wrote another, which is romantic instead of classical, and therefore broader-based. It places man in his cosmos, passing from the stars through animals and plants to man as an organism set in an environment and enveloped in tradition. Only the last half of the work tells man's story as preserved in his history.

For their day, these eighteenth-century products are not too different from Wells' twentieth-century *Outline of History*.

I pass over also another kind of philosophy of history, that of Hegel, which, instead of narrating, summarizing, and commenting, uses history to extract from it such facts as will illustrate one main principle. It was an influential work and is still interesting to read, but it is scarcely relevant to an inquiry into the natural history of civilizations, let alone into the nature of style.

Regretfully, I also pass by Northrop's *The Meeting of East and West*, 1946. In spite of stimulating insights, it also does not purport to be a natural history of civilizations. It revolves around a dualism of principles, selects its illustrative data, and is slanted by the desire to head off world catastrophe.

So much, then, for "philosophies" of history.

Definitely symptomatic of a positivist approach to our subject is an attempt by Quételet, the Belgian founder of the formal statistical approach in science. In his *Social System and its Laws*, 1848, he calculates (on pages 158–164) the average duration of five ancient "empires," according to the chronologies then available to him. Thus "Assyria" lasted from Assur "grandson" of Noah in B.C. 2347 to the fall of Nineveh in 767 (*sic*), or 1580 years; the "empire" of the Jews ran from Joshua, 1451 B.C., to A.D. 71, or 1522 years; that of Greece from the Athenian kingdom in B.C. 1556 to 146, or 1410 years. The average of the five cases is 1461 years; which, Quételet comments, is also the great Sothic year of the Egyptian calendar and the life span of the phoenix. I am inclined to add with a grave face that the standard deviation of the five cases computes to 185 years, or nearly 8 per cent of the mean.

However, several straws from the history of thought are blowing around this bit of solemn naïveté. First, the approach is as positivist, empirical, exploratory as its result is premature and meaningless. Second, while the talk is of "empires," this concept was on the one hand already present in Gibbons' famous *Decline and Fall;* and on the other it is germinal to the "civilizations" of a generation or two later. Third, it is assumed that these empires have comparable durations; and the average of these is actually about what Spengler and Toynbee and others have come out with. Fourth, when the positivist Quételet says that "all organized beings traverse the cycle of their existence while showing nearly the same phases," he is, for all his quantifying, expressing both the idea of repetitive parallelism and the core of the organicist analogy.

In short, we have here an early statistician blandly uttering thoughts which were accepted not only by Spengler seventy years later but also by Danilevsky and Toynbee, whom I am about to discuss. My point is that what the statistician already said and believed in 1848 cannot be specially distinctive of these later men—it is part of an older climate of thought that continued into the time in which they were born.

Nikolai Danilevsky was born at Moscow in 1822 and died in 1885 at Tiflis. He was trained in natural science, specialized in botany, and became a governmental expert in fisheries. He was an ardent Panslavist, and in 1865–1867 wrote *Russia and Europe*, which was published in 1869 in the periodical *Zara* (*Zaria*), "Dawn," and issued in book form in 1871 and again later. Danilevsky was a genuine patriot, and the purpose of his book was to prepare his countrymen for a future struggle with Europe, from which not only would they emerge victorious but would then take over the civilization of the world. He proceeded to base this prediction on a review of the history of the world's civilizations.

A programmatic partisanship such as his seems unpromising as an instigation to sound historical interpretation. But Danilevsky had the advantage of habits of impartiality from his natural science training; and he did formulate the problem of the nature and succession of civilizations in approximately the form it was to maintain until today. He was trained in comparing, as historians were not. As a Cuvierian biologist, he was still interested in classification and in basing his classification on fundamental types of total organization. Remaining a non-Darwinian, he was exempt from the danger of being swept off his feet, as for instance the early anthropologists were swept off, into extending the new theory of evolution into a simple linear progressivism of culture; nor did he try to apply to civilizations a survival-of-the-fittest formula. Again, his natural history background kept him clear of any one overriding formula, such as a Hegel, Comte, Spencer, or Bergson would seek. Apparently it did not occur to him to look for one fundamental principle on which to rest the victory of his beloved Russia. He validated this coming triumph of Russia by data taken from the specific relation of Europe and Russia, without much warping his interpretation of other civilizations. In consequence he developed an outline theory which was unencumbered by emotional preconceptions or complicating excess of detail, and was based on a sensible, reasonable presentation of summarized historical data. It has been called a pedestrian formulation, and in a sense it is such; but there lies its strength. And within its frame, Spengler, Toynbee, Sorokin, and the rest of us could emphasize, elaborate, and rear special superstructures.

Danilevsky's general theory was slow in coming to the world's attention. It occupied only about a sixth of his book, the remainder of which was frankly pro-Russian propaganda that would have antagonized Europeans; whereas most Russians that read the volume would have been little interested in the nonpropagandist theory. The book sold rather slowly in Russia, the reprintings being limited to the years between 1888 and 1895; and it was not translated out of Russian until a partial German version by Nötzel was issued in 1920 as a result of the furore over Spengler. This translation included only about half of the original, but the motivation of its publication ensured inclusion of all its general theory. My direct knowledge of Danilevsky is based on this translation; my indirect, on what Sorokin and Stuart Hughes tell about him.

Danilevsky recognizes that there have been until now a dozen autonomous civilizations, which he calls "culture-historical types." There is only the one exemplar of each "type." These twelve are the same as Spengler's eight (partly under somewhat different names), with Iranian, Hebrew, and Peruvian added and Spengler's Classic split into separate Greek and Roman. They correspond to Cuvier's biological types—which modern biologists call phyla or subkingdoms and now view historically as well as classificatorily. According to Danilevsky, the fundamental types of life and the culture-historical types or civilizations correspond in having each a basic plan of organization which is separate and distinctive. We have here the core of Spengler's dogmatic intuitive thought, but expressed fifty years earlier by a systematic biologist looking at human history as a whole. It is uncertain whether Spengler was influenced by Danilevsky, or even knew of him; but the parallelism is certainly striking.

Moreover, Danilevsky goes on, the people of each "type" independently worked out a basic principle for their civilization, which thenceforward remained isolated from others. The civilizations could pass on their achievements to one another—but only like food to animals or fertilizer to plants; the culture-wholes did not themselves blend or hybridize. Peoples like Huns or Mongols are destructive in role, hastening the disintegration of dying civilizations. Wholly nonhistorical peoples are only "ethnographic material," which may increase the richness of the great culture types but never attains to a historic individuality of its own.

Danilevsky lists several "laws" that govern civilizations. Three of these refer to the linguistic, ethnic, and political conditions most favorable to the rise and perpetuation of a civilization. The most important law is that the fundamental plan (*Grundlagen*) of a civilization is not transmissible, although it may be modified by influences from others. The fifth law says that civilizations can be very long in developing, but that their flowering is brief and exhausts them once and for all—like a century plant. On the basis of several examples, Danilevsky seems to conclude that the florescence lasts at most a matter of some centuries.

After that, the society "rests on its oars" in Toynbee's phrase, becomes apathetic in idealization of its past; or it runs into contradictions which show its plan to have been inadequate, and hence lead to despair. But if nevertheless the society manages to survive, the despair may turn into complacent self-infatuation. His examples are China, late Rome, Byzantium.

While the Danilevsky scheme thus sees civilizations as fated to die after fruiting, he rates them as coming to the peak of their potence earlier than to the summit of their achievement; after the latter, inevitable decline ensues. The idea of growth and life cycle is clear.

He sees European—or as he calls it, Germano-Romanic—civilization at its aesthetic and intellectual acme around 1500–1700, with scientific applications, technology, and wealth delayed in their culmination until the nineteenth century. However, the dry rot has begun, and Europe will inevitably be replaced by Russia, which has husbanded or conserved its energies, so that its flowering still lies ahead.

The earliest civilizations were too occupied with establishing themselves to achieve anything very differentiated. Later ones excelled respectively in religion, in culture in the narrower sense, or in politics. Europe was the first to rise high in two fields, the economic and the cultural. But Russia gives evidence, from its temper to date, of achieving supremacy in three areas: religion, politics, and culture, when its time comes.

In his generic theory Danilevsky made three main assumptions. The first was that each major civilization was a sort of archetype, distinctive, unmergeable, and built on a master plan of its own. This is based on analogy with pre-Darwinian biology, but so far as I know Danilevsky was the first to apply the idea to human history and culture, preceding Spengler by a half century. It is a definitely pluralistic but non-cyclic view.

Second, he held that civilizations have a limited life and replace each other. This is the old rise-and-fall-of-empire notion, which is cyclic in at least one sense of the word. Danilevsky's contribution here was to refocus the relevance of the idea from empires to civilizations. He was ready to use the notion in favor of Russia of the future, but he remained vague about the past, certainly being more interested in the stages and processes of a civilization's life than in its chronological duration or regularity.

Third, he held that the inductive, comparative study of the particular qualities as well as the common qualities of civilizations would lead to a larger understanding of history.

The first and the third of these ideas were new; and he changed the focus of the second.

After Danilevsky, the only other pretence of a systematic effort in the field in the nineteenth century is an American one: Brooks Adams' *The Law of Civilization and Decay*, 1895/1896. Although it has retained some nominal repute (it was reprinted in 1943), one cannot but wonder whether it was really taken seriously by scholarly opinion in the United States sixty years ago, other than for the ancestry of its author. The laws, summarily expounded, mix eighteenth-century mechanical and nineteenth-century biological metaphors with immemorially homespun psychology about fear and greed. The main text, after a bit on the Romans, consists of ten chapters each discussing some limited episode in European history from "the Middle Age" to modern centralization, strung together on a thread of how the "energy" amassed by emotional and martial man was dissipated by economic competition. It seems a confused book written in immature despair. Perhaps,

> Und weil mein Fässchen trübe läuft,
> So ist die Welt auch auf der Neige.

> "Because my little vat is running murky,
> I see the world too down to its lees."

Except for one or two much younger men, Arnold Toynbee is the only historian by profession who has seriously occupied himself with the comparison of civilizations. This concern has earned him little sympathy among his professional colleagues; rather, suspicion, wide uneasiness, disbelief: a sort of disapproval of his wanting to push things so far.

I shall treat of him as briefly as I can, not out of disrespect, but because his doctrine is widely known in comparison with most others.

Toynbee's stature is so large that it would be unfair to call him a Spenglerian. But he has been influenced by Spengler—as I too have been. Stuart Hughes includes him among the "New Spenglerians." Toynbee himself has told how when he first read Spengler he wondered whether he had not been anticipated, but decided that English empiricism might go farther than German *a priori*.[1]

*The Study of History*—1934, 1939, 1954—runs to ten volumes as against Spengler's two, and is elaborately organized. The title is appropriate: it is indeed an interpretation of all known history so far as relevant to the understanding of civilizations. Toynbee's knowledge is vast. It is both continuous and coherent, where Spengler's was fitful.

The rise-and-fall concept, analogous to organic growth and decay, is as basic in Toynbee as in Spengler. They both derived it from the intellectual atmosphere of the century or century and a half that preceded them: witness my previous remarks on Gibbon, Adelung, and Quételet. The beginning and the end of the courses interest Toynbee most. He divides the course of each civilization into Genesis, Growth, Breakdown, and Dis-

[1] *Civilization on Trial* (1948), pp. 9–10.

integration. Within the original six volumes, Genesis gets one volume and a half, Growth one (the slenderest), Breakdown one, and Disintegration two, and those long. In the Somervell Abridgment, there are more pages on Disintegration than on the three preceding stages combined. Toynbee is not a prophet of doom, but he does consider and almost preach about how, and how only, our civilization may be saved.

It is expectable for a historian to be interested in events, and Toynbee's emphasis on beginning and end is in line with this. For each civilization the challenge that gave it birth is defined; also, its time of troubles, its church, its universal state, its universal peace, and the end—all of them large events. It is the life history of a "society," usually something much bigger than a nation, but tending toward a single empire. This society is held together by its civilization. But the culture itself, as something substantive, is hardly examined by Toynbee except incidentally; its specific quality is scarcely portrayed; least of all is it viewed as a style or possible assemblage of styles. How far clocks and credit and cathedrals and counterpoint may have been immanently connected in our civilization, as Spengler proclaimed with vehemence, or how far their association was secondary and partly fortuitous—this sort of problem which I have already discussed, Toynbee does not deal with.

It seems to me that his *Study* emanates from orthodox history, mainly political but based on a good modern foundation of social considerations, heavily tinctured with considerations of morality. After all, the *Study* is not so far from Gibbon's *Decline and Fall* in theme and manner. True, Toynbee has treated ascent as well as decline, and he has treated them twenty-one times. Unfortunately this twenty-one times appears to be precisely what has alarmed his fellow historians: they smell a formula that repeats, and mostly they will have none of it.

I cannot quarrel with the historians, since I have spent sixty years learning to distrust formulae in my own field of ethnology and culture history. But my sympathy is all with Toynbee for seeing a larger problem, having the courage to march up to it, and wrestling with it with suppleness and tenacity and enormous resource of insight.

I should say his main trouble is that he has explained too much. There is not enough left unaccounted for. The pattern fits too many instances at too many points. The better Toynbee argues his way around discrepancies from uniformity, the less convinced do his colleagues become: they assume that regularity just cannot be so great in the events of history. Personally, I find Toynbee particularly stimulating and satisfactory when he is dealing with the societies that failed to achieve the standard pattern—his abortive and arrested civilizations.

On the other hand, the historians might well be more tolerant of his unorthodoxy, which is after all considerably a matter of degree. Empire, revolution, universal state, heroic age, warbands, proletariats, city states— these are all concepts that they too use. That he has added some new ideas and terms is no great matter for alarm, especially as some of these are productive, like the chrysalis religion as being that which helps form new civilizations out of old. The main difference is rather that Toynbee has used the concepts systematically—and twenty-one times. Perhaps the number really is a bit steep; especially as he finds most of the twenty-one to have had a pretty fair fit. But if historians as a group refuse to deal with concepts unless these have had a name in good literary standing for most of a century, and refuse to make comparisons outside the particular civilization which is their field, except possibly now and then with an "apparented" one, they run some risk of finding themselves before long in an old-fogey position. The alternatives are not limited to swallowing Toynbee's system whole or walking past it looking sidelong. Coulborn has shown, dealing with the narrower case of feudal institutions viewed comparatively, that it is possible to find civilizations that fit and contain a certain institutional type, others that partly fit, still others that do not fit at all.[2] Toynbee has faced a large problem with devotion and sincerity and has deployed upon it an almost incredible learning. He would seem to have earned a dispassionate professional analysis of his better and his worse, of what are his permanent contributions and what his misfires: an appraisal on the order of the one that Eduard Meyer gave Spengler, and proportionally fuller as the *Study* is the larger work.[3]

[2] See note 9 below in this chapter.

[3] This larger appraisal may actually have been made in a recent article in *Ethics*, LXIV (1956), 235–244, by R. Coulborn: "Fact and Fiction in Toynbee's *Study of History*."

The twenty-one civilizations—or by another count twenty-nine—evidence Toynbee's desire to do thorough justice to his subject. Their classification is a bit complicated for those who are not experts in the comparative. But at least he has got beyond using the obvious or popular array as Spengler and Danilevsky have done. Some of the names are formidable; but some new names are taxonomically necessary as soon as it is decided that an earlier and a later culture in the same area have more significant distinguishing features than uniting ones. Hence Toynbee's Sinic and Far Eastern, Indic and Hindu, Sumeric and Babylonic. These do *not* have quite the same import as Chinese I and II, Indian I and II, Mesopotamian I and II would have on the basis of Egyptian I, II, III, IV. The unfamiliar names may worry the innocent a bit, but to the historian they mean that new and fundamental choices have been considered and made. As I said fourteen years ago, this matter of the number and classification of the cultures dealt with may look like mere systematizing for its own sake, and it necessarily rests on the evaluation of masses of technical evidence; but nevertheless it touches every important aspect of the history of civilizations.[4] Toynbee's elaborate roster is not in the least a device for impressing those of less learning. It is worked out and justified with full sincerity and much toil. It is in reciprocation of that spirit that I shall now point out some of the weaknesses.

The Syriac civilization seems as artificial as Spengler's Magian, for reasons stated in Appendix I. The distinc-

[4] Review, reprinted in *The Nature of Culture* (1952).

tions between Syriac and its successors, Iranic and Arabic which merge into Islamic, are tenuous. There are five separate Christian civilizations, two of them abortive; which seems unnecessarily many, even though each had its church. On some of these out-of-the-way minor civilizations, like the early Irish and Scandinavian, the Osmanli and the Nomad, Toynbee is intrinsically superb; his arbitrariness is in choosing to include these cases because of some partial fit to a scheme of events, but excluding others that are perhaps not abortive or are less arrested. To select the few thousand Spartans of tiny Laconia and count them as a unit counterbalancing the whole of Hellenic society of which they were so manifestly a part suggests that the point of "challenge and response"—an essentially moral factor—which Toynbee has set up as a criterion of genesis of civilizations, weighs more heavily in his reckoning than the whole substance and quality of the culture of the challenged and responding society.

Similarly as regards inclusion of Polynesians and Eskimos among the arrested civilizations. Surely the long sea voyages of the one group, and the living on ice through the arctic winter by part of the other, are dramatic responses indicating high courage. But is such a moral trait really enough on which to base the distinctness of one of the world's twenty-nine civilizations, full and arrested? The natives of the northwest coast of America built themselves a far richer and more varied culture than the Eskimo, on as specialized a subsistence basis of sea foods as the Eskimo. In fact, this was probably the most elaborate, original, and highly stylized of all cultures that did wholly without farming or herding and that hunted and gathered but little on land. Is this Northwest Coast culture, which achieved so much more before its "arrest," to be excluded simply because its society settled in a less harsh environment than the Eskimo and then proceeded to orginate a much more notable body of culture?

And how about our Pueblo Indians, farmers at the margin of the desert, with their culture of so much more content and more definite form than all their neighbors? They never formed a state, it is true; but they did achieve a "church." Or how about the Yoruba or any one of a dozen larger nationalities in West Africa, or the group of them together, with their metalwork, kingdoms, developed law, and penetrating religion? There seems something capricious in wholly omitting such peoples when Polynesians and Eskimos are admitted to have have had at least an arrested civilization.

I do not believe Toynbee is capricious. I give him full credit for a sense of responsibility, and for realizing that a systematic study of the civilizations in history must operate with a roster of cultures that is reasonably justifiable. He was the first to abandon the older common-knowledge grouping and to lead us into a realm of consideration which involved new taxonomic problems, but which also held promise of a natural classification that would serve as a basis for growing future understandings. Why then did he leave his classification inconsistent and incomplete?

I think the reason is that Toynbee did not really try to classify civilizations as cultures. By cultures I mean aggregations of a certain specific culture content structured in patterns, the word civilizations merely denoting the larger and more massive or important examples of cultures. Instead of this, I again see Toynbee's civilizations resolving largely into societies; even though they are societies usually or potentially greater than nations or states, and thus more significant. They are not societies viewed as living and feeling in a certain characteristic unitary way which is described. They are viewed as societies of men interacting with one another and their environment. They perform acts—acts of courage or self-sufficiency or leadership or selfishness or withdrawal or response to challenge. These acts result in the kind of events that old-fashioned historians have narrated for two or three thousand years, with the difference that the historians told primarily about individual men, Toynbee of groups of men—minorities, proletarians, warbands, barbarians, whole societies. When we reflect on it, there is relatively little said by Toynbee about the specific kind of culture these groups lived in and under while performing their acts.

It is not that Toynbee is blind to culture. He is an extraordinarily cultured person, and is sensitive, even poetic. He is also open and eager for the broadest view, the widest range of knowledge, the value of comparison. But, as the title of his work says, he is literally examining, even though summarily through societies, the actions of men. His subject matter is still basically that of orthodox history, though his treatment is distinctive and broader. His "civilizations" are societies, not cultures. They are large societies whose success and failure he analyzes in terms of—what? In terms of the layman's everyday psychology viewed moralistically. There is still much of Gibbon in Toynbee, though he is not cynical and he is modern in having transcended ethnocentricity. The charge that he has a mediaeval mind is untrue and unfair. But it is an old-fashioned mind—deliberately and willingly old-fashioned in founding its system of the ultimate interpretation of human history on explanations through character and morals. Therefore the distinctive and differential qualities of his civilizations are largely missed or ignored (least so for the abortive and arrested ones), in spite of the profoundity of his knowledge and the wide balance of his comparisons.

It would be unfair to blame Toynbee for doing something different from what I would have tried to do had I been he. It is, however, important to recognize his aim and method for what they actually are. They are completely different from Spengler's: the two men share little beyond the fact of making comparisons, the belief that peoples and their civilizations tend to run a set course, and a concern with our future. Spengler is dealing with cultures, and is delineating them contrastively, without inquiring into what made them as they are. Toynbee is concerned with the comparative uniformities in the life histories of societies and with the psychological and moral factors that determine the courses of these histories.

Other than Toynbee, most historians have shrunk from systematically entering the field of comparison.

The late R. G. Collingwood in his illuminating and elegant *The Idea of History*, 1946, maintains the conservative point of view.[5] I agree with his criticisms of Spengler (who is easy to criticize), but I note he has nothing at all good to say about him. Perhaps Spengler had antagonized Collingwood by his sniping at history and historians.

Of more general interest is what Collingwood has to say about historical cycles or periods. He calls them fabrications, due to some luminous point engaging someone's interest, by which fact the period or cycle is given a seeming beginning and end. But these boundaries are illusory in that they represent comparative ignorance on the part of the investigator. A period can always be compared with another one, which it will resemble "in being a period"—and apparently, according to Collingwood, only in that. He thus sees the cyclical view as merely a function of the limitations of knowledge. A period or cycle begins and ends with the end and beginning of our ignorance. History is always being seen in cycles, but they are always illusory, because organization of knowledge will forever shift and dissolve.[6]

[5] Also two earlier articles in *Antiquity*, I (1929), 311–325, 435–446.

[6] This is not only with reference to Spengler. In *The Idea of History*, p. 328, he speaks generically. "The old dogma of a single historical progress leading to the present, and the modern dogma of historical cycles, that is, of a multiple progress leading to 'great ages' and then to decadence, are thus mere projections of the historian's ignorance upon the screen of the past."

I leave this profound negativism to historians to accept or reject, but it prompts me to a remark on the concept of cycle.

The cyclic concept is widely considered to be of basic importance in the work of Spengler, Toynbee, and others here dealt with. The reader may have realized that until this chapter I have had very little to say about it. This has been deliberate.

The word cycle has several meanings. There is no quarreling with the special sense, as in the business cycle or the sunspot cycle, which refers to repetitive variability in phenomena which can be handled and given significance by quantitative expression. Other than that, the word cycle seems intellectually imprecise. Sometimes it is used to denote exact repetition; sometimes irregularly spaced and partial repetition; sometimes merely similar but separate courses (as for Spengler's cultures); sometimes nothing more than the duration of something, as in "a cycle of Cathay." And it is a word particularly liable to carrying a heavy emotional charge: witness all the dwelling on crisis, decay, death, doom, and extinction associated with the so-called cyclic view.

I am aware that the historic concept of style which I have been developing implies limitation, transience, and perhaps mortality. It may be that preoccupation with style has made me impervious to cycle. But at least a style cannot be repeated—it is too individual and unique. Another style may take its place, and may run a generically similar course; but they differ so substantively in quality that it would be farfetched to speak of their relation as cyclic. Styles always are concrete. But cycle is a concept that runs easily into the cloudy.

I will add that those who have had most to say about what is so often referred to as cycles in history, have tended to avoid the word. This holds for Danilevsky, Spengler, and Toynbee.

Rushton Coulborn, apart from some pregnant criticisms and journal articles,[7] has had in preparation for some time a systematic book, or rather two, on the origin of civilization and on the repetitive rise and fall of civilized societies, of which he has published only a hint or foretaste.[8] In addition, he has brought out a comparative study of feudalism, 1956, which, though it does not compare whole civilizations, does compare the appearance of one institution in a series of them.[9] More accurately it is an inquiry into the appearance or nonappearance of feudalism, or the degree of its appearance; this on the basis of a series of definitions of feudalism and a series of essays by specialists reviewing the seeming or

[7] Such as "Civilized and Primitive Culture," *Phylon*, VIII (1947), 274–285; "Note on Method in Anthropology," *SW Journ. Anthrop.*, I (1945), 311–317; "Causes in Culture," *Am. Anthrop.*, LIV (1952), 112–116. See also footnote 3.

[8] On his views on the origin of civilization, see "Survival of the Fittest in the Atomic Age," *Ethics*, LVII (1947), 238–244; on uniformities in history as part of the rise and fall of civilizations, see *ibid.*, pp. 245–246, and *Feudalism in History* (1956) edited and partly written by Coulborn, pp. 364–365, 388–394.

[9] *Feudalism in History*, pp. 183–397.

alleged feudal phenomena in the history of nine countries in Eurasia.

Coulborn finds only two fully proven cases of feudalism, those in Western Europe and Japan. In Chou China and middle-era Mesopotamia feudalism probably existed. In late dynastic Egypt and in Rajput India there were starts toward feudalism which were interfered with from outside. There are several more possible cases not treated of in the book or in the conference that preceded its writing; of these, Coulborn considers one certain, namely, Korea. A half-dozen instances, in which there is semblance of feudalism or it has been alleged, are decided negatively by him. There is thus no finding of compulsive regularity. Feudalism is a mode of revival of a disintegrated society and its culture, either within a broken-down empire or in adjacent territory. But empires and civilizations can decline without feudalism ensuing; and at least as often as not, it does not ensue.

From this case-by-case empirical testing of feudalism, Coulborn goes on to outline sketchily his provisional theory of comparative culture history.[10] This theory sees in decline and revival of civilizations (note the inversion of "rise and fall," or "growth and death") one of the major recurrent processes of history. He sees religion as the greatest agency in the revival: it is a special form of culture developed by men when they face the decline of their society and culture. The decline begins intellectually, invades art, and reaches politics. Thereafter feudalism may develop; if so, it meets the rising

[10] "Conclusion," *ibid.*, sect. 10.

tide of religion, and the two operate together for a time toward a new civilization and to extend this to a wider range of peoples hitherto barbarian. This idea seems more generalized than Toynbee's fruitful chrysalis religion concept. Coulborn goes on to raise the question—which he admits cannot as yet be answered—whether feudalism or something like it may not have been even more influential in the genesis of civilization than in its revivals.

The present is not the occasion to amplify or discuss these suggestions, beyond roughly placing them in context. It is to be hoped Coulborn will soon extend and evidence his views.

Even less can I say about a completed but unpublished book of which I have seen only an outline, by a still younger man, Philip Bagby, technically an anthropologist, which I mention because it falls in the same historico-cultural stream of thought as Coulborn's.[11]

The Russian-born Pitirim Sorokin is the only sociologist who has entered the field.[12] Some of his views cut squarely across those of most students of comparative history and civilizations. Rather than mangle Sorokin's philosophy by an undue reduction, I have put my detailed analysis of him into Appendix III, and shall only outline here what the issues are that his special approach raises.

Sorokin denies that civilizations are historic entities.

[11] The present title is *Culture and History*. See also a clear article, "Culture and the Causes of Culture," *Am. Anthrop.*, LV (1953), 535–554.

[12] His works are cited in Appendix III.

This recalls Collingwood's denial that periods and "cycles" in history have reality. To Sorokin, civilizations are accidental and unintegrated assemblages—not meaningful systems but mere vast congeries, to use a word he is fond of. This in turn suggests Lowie's utterance to which I have already alluded, about "that planless hodge-podge, that thing of shreds and patches called civilization." However, the context of the phrase, which occurs in the last paragraph of his *Primitive Society* of 1920, shows that Lowie was thinking of the *origin* of the content of civilizations rather than of their nature. Also, in more than thirty years he has not developed his passing remark into a systematically negative view.

Sorokin denies both causal and meaningful integration to civilizations. They do not grow, they have no life history, they do not die. Here he is the antithesis of Spengler, whose cultures are completely and foreordainedly integrated: they even begin with a fate. I think Sorokin has slipped into the contrary overstatement, perhaps through being more interested in certain conceptualizations of his own than in civilizations as mere happenings in history. I am confident that not only Toynbee, Coulborn, and Danilevsky but practically all historians and anthropologists take the intermediate view: that civilizations are partially integrated. Much that is foreign keeps flowing into them, but it is gradually assimilated and co-ordinated. I have several times said here that such integration as civilizations have must never be regarded as primary, but as something that they accomplish as they live along. Just so, most students would no doubt admit that while civilizations are somewhat difficult to delimit, and while there may never be unanimous agreement on a right scheme for delimiting them (much as with historic periods, or with phyla in biology), nevertheless common sense demands that we accept civilizations as units naturally given in history.

Sorokin does grant meaningful integration to at least part of what he calls "cultural systems," by which he denotes natural segments of human culture, such as language, religion, fine art, and so on. He also attributes integration to "supersystems." These are a formulation of his own. He calls them the grand forms in which culture appears. I would rather phrase them as pervasive qualities that predominate for a time in a culture, and are then replaced by another quality. Sorokin has traced in voluminous detail his three (or four) supersystems through over three thousand years of Mediterranean and Western history. We can accordingly be sure, from this analyzed evidence, of following what his concepts actually mean concretely. Mainly, the supersystems appear in a great pendulum-pulsation between the "Ideational" and the "Sensate" form. There is also a brief "Idealistic synthesis," falling between Ideational and Sensate, and a brief "Eclectic incoherence" after Sensate and before Ideational.

Analysis of Sorokin's chronology, as well as of his cited characterizing items, makes it quite clear that his "Ideational supersystem" corresponds to the early or rising period of cultures; the Sensate, to their maturity and decline; with the Idealistic tallying with the culmination (especially in art and philosophy), and the incoherent Eclectic with the interregna or Dark Ages between large cultures. For the tracing out of this correspondence I refer to Appendix III.

Sorokin has himself indicated that he sees similarity between the courses of his supersystems and the courses of civilizations. I suspect his denial of integration and reality to civilizations will prove to be a function of his preferring a systematizing approach over the historic approach followed by almost all other workers in the field. The issue should therefore be adjudicable without bloodshed. On other main points Sorokin seems in essential agreement with the rest of us.

# 6

# The Art Approach to Civilizations; Conclusions

BEFORE summing up the somewhat wide-ranging ideas and interpretations that I have presented, there is one other topic that calls for comment.

This is a set of findings, mainly by theoreticians or historians of the arts, on regularities and recurrences in the field of art, sometimes extending also into the rest of civilization. These views will bring us back close to the subject of style with which we began; although I was then considering mainly how far the concept of style could be developed as a useful tool, whereas the writers to whom we now come rather take style for granted but elaborate its internal and comparative behavior.

This group of scholars raises problems of several kinds. One of these problems is contrastive polarities. Another deals with recurrent rhythms, back and forth movements between extremes. Then there is the matter of recurrences of subject, treatment, or manner in more or less corresponding stages of the arts of distinct civilizations. And finally we have the theory that the arts themselves appear in a particular order and time sequence in different civilizations.

Under contrastive polarities, we have pairs like classic and romantic, or idealistic and realistic, or ethos and pathos. These terms generally originated in endeavors to denote the typical products of a phase of style. The terms were then often extended either to other arts in the same civilization or to the same art in other civilizations. Thus literature, painting, and music all are said to have gone "romantic" in early nineteenth-century Europe; whereas classic stages are recognized in Latin literature of the time of Augustus, in French of the seventeenth century, and in English of the eighteenth.

Usage is, however, quite loose, and the terms must be employed with caution. Thus the French and English classic or Augustan periods of literature imply a definite element of restriction, whereas the original Augustan in Rome did not—in fact the term here refers to little else than the culmination of excellence for the whole of Latin literature. Applied to European music, classic again refers primarily to culmination, but sometimes has the more specific sense of pre-expressionist; not to mention the nonhistorical and commercial sense of the word, when classic is contrasted with non-high-standard, popular, or vulgar music.

Some of these contrastive pairs overlap quite largely in their connotation, and yet each possesses overtones of its own. Such are classic-romantic, ethos-pathos, the Apollinian-Dionysian of Nietzsche and Apollinian-Faustian of Spengler, and the ideational-sensate of Sorokin.

Frank Chambers published in 1928 a remarkable little book called *Cycles of Taste*,[1] the point of which is that while art was becoming great in both ancient Greece and again in Europe, it was unconscious of mission and function; it was often anonymous because there was little interest in the artist's individuality as compared with his product; and moralists feared art. With the peak reached or passed, there came, on the contrary, a consciousness of art, of beauty as such, of art for art's sake. Collectors and connoisseurs appeared, also critics and dilettantes; there began a cult of greatness and of personality.

We might well call the two periods Creative and Conscious. But to do so would convert an actual gradual development into a telling but oversimplified dichotomy of little precise historic applicability. Chambers sees the Gothic period as much like fifth-century Athens in its attributes. This would leave the Renaissance as the counterpart of the Hellenistic-Roman course, whereas in fact nineteenth-century art seems the closer counterpart of Hellenistic in its attitudes. So far as visual art is con-

[1] It was followed in 1932 by *The History of Taste*.

cerned, its Greek culmination would fall in the Creative
half of the polarity, the European culmination in the
Conscious half; which does seem imprecise.

Those who deal with recurrent rhythms generally also
make use of polarities between which the pendulum
swings back and forth. The durations may be as long as
eras or as short as generations.

Curt Sachs, eminent musicologist and high authority
on the history of musical instruments, published in 1946
*The Commonwealth of Art: Style in the Fine Arts, Mu-
sic, and the Dance.* The last part of the volume essays the
problem of how styles grow and change. The mechanism
of organization is by the qualities of ethos and pathos.
Ethos expressses perfection, permanence, serenity, strict-
ness, and moderation; but pathos, passion, suffering,
freedom, and exaggeration. Ethos and pathos are not
states, according to Sachs, but opposite directions in
which style flows like a tide. To a large extent a given
moment of style expresses predominant ethos or pathos
not in its nature but by contrast with the generation
preceding.[2]

Following out this idea, Sachs sees the last five centuries of the combined arts of Western Europe (excepting literatures, which are nationally bound by speech)
as characterized by alternating predominance of ethos
and pathos. He specifies fourteen such flows, seven each
way. This yields an average duration of around thirty-

[2] Page 334.

five years, about three to a century, or a generation as it used to be estimated.

These generational tides group by fours into Renaissance, Baroque, Romanticism, Naturalism, beginning respectively about 1430, 1600, 1760, and 1890; and these larger groups again alternately incline toward ethos and pathos. But the first two groups can be combined into a sort of Greater Renaissance and the last two into a Greater Romanticism, which again contrast in relative ethos and pathos. We can even take all the foregoing as one grand unit of later European art and contrast it with earlier—with pre-1400, ancient and mediaeval art combined—and it will be perceptible, according to Sachs, that in comparison with each other, ethos prevails in the earlier, pathos in the later era.

I would admit that, granted use of the ethos-pathos polarity, the drift would be seen by most people as moving in the direction claimed; and the same for the subdivisions. But I do not know what the meaning of this drift is, unless it be that it takes centuries for the arts to learn and master to the full the degree of emotion they can express.

As for the generation-length fluctuations, I am more in doubt. It must be difficult to measure or even estimate such minor qualitative fluctuations in several arts at once. And even if established, the fluctuations would be only superficial modulations, like the dress-skirt length tidal swings with which I began consideration of style. And in the longer view of whole cultures, it is their "mean sea-level" that concerns us most—even though if there are diurnal fluctuations we shall want to know these also.

Paul Ligeti, a student of architecture, in 1926 published in Hungarian a book of which only the 1931 German version, *Der Weg aus dem Chaos* ("The Way out of Chaos") is available to most of us in this country. It deals primarily with the visual arts of Europe. The illustrations are very aptly chosen; and diagrams abound.

Ligeti also recognizes oscillations, which he calls waves. He finds seven between 910 and 1910, varying between 120 and 170 years in length, and averaging 140. He counts from trough to trough, and the troughs are low points at which there is turn-over of manner. In France the low points came at 910, 1080, 1220, 1370, 1530, 1650, 1780, 1910; in Germany, from twenty to sixty years later. The first three waves embrace Romanesque and Gothic art; the Renaissance and Baroque occupy the next two and a half; Rococo, Classicism, "Renaissancism," and Impressionism crowd into the remaining one and a half waves.

The Ligeti waves have nothing to do with the Sachs waves. They seem independent of each other as regards stylistic content, duration, and absolute chronology; even though four of Sachs's generation-length tides just about equal the average length of Ligeti's waves.

As for recurrences in diverse styles and civilizations, there are really two sets of phenomena involved: the independent appearance of certain qualities in noncorresponding phases of different styles; and their appearance in corresponding phases. The first class would presumably be accidental, in the sense that a quality or manner, such as say, impressionism, being one of a limited number of possible manners in painting, would have a certain limited degree of likelihood of appearing in the painting of any culture, but its place in the development of that art would be haphazard, being dependent on a variety of contingencies. In the second case, the stylistic quality or trait would be construed as due to factors immanent in a scheme of development or growth of styles generally: something as a toddling gait is a function of infancy, tumultuousness of adolescence, a stooping body of age. This second class would presumably have more significance for most of us, as partaking more nearly of a law or predetermination. But it is important to distinguish the two classes, just because it remains to be proved that there really exists in styles some degree of predetermination. This proof can be brought only by accumulating a sufficient number of genuinely parallel instances that are independent of one another, and by making sure that they are not of the first or contingent class through ascertaining that their occurrence really falls at corresponding places within their styles.

For instance, Ligeti, in dealing with the quality of impressionism, points out that this appears not only in late nineteenth-century painting but in the work of the great Japanese Sesshu of the fifteenth century. This similarity of quality is easy to recognize; but when the New Empire Egyptian profile portraits of the Akhnaton reformation, in low stone relief, are also cited, the difference in medium and therefore technique makes the parallelism less convincing.

On the other hand, Ligeti sees a phase of impressionism arising repeatedly toward the end of each wave of painting, just before its trough or low point. He cites del Sarto and Correggio before 1530, Hals, Rembrandt, and Velazquez before 1650, Guardi and Goya before 1780, and the conventional "school" of impressionists in France in the forty years preceding 1910. I consider the likenesses indubitable: the loss of linearity by breaking of the bounding line into blur, the representation of the illumination on things rather than of the surfaces of things in themselves, with consequent interest in space, leading in extreme cases to preoccupation with intervening atmosphere instead of object. However, Ligeti's point of correspondence is of course proved only if he can independently establish the existence of his 140-year waves, and their beginning at the dates he alleges. Also, there is something like impressionistic technique and feeling apparent in Watteau, who worked about 1715 at the crest of the alleged 1650–1780 wave instead of just before a trough, and who thus violates the asserted rhythmic regularity of periodicity.

It is evident that we shall have no certainty and little probability in such opinions while they rest on judgments that are themselves impressionistic. To be convincing, the evidence will have to be precisely definable, both as to the facts under immediate consideration and as to their entire phenomenal matrix; and due weight will also have to be given to facts contrary to the generalization being tested.

On the other hand there are certain roughhewn qualities of stage of development first recognized in architecture and sculpture that have been pretty widely accepted for the arts generally: I believe, because they commend themselves by a common-sense likelihood. For instance, a style would hardly begin with a rococo or Churrigueresque or flamboyant stage: some basic structure has to be developed before superstructural detail. A simple frontal posture and a fixed stare and smile not only fit our expectation of what a technically inexperienced style of sculpture might produce, but are actually found in incipient styles—and in those that suffered arrest while immature.[3]

Waldemar Deonna has been particularly successful in piling up illustrations of striking instances of specific similarities in corresponding phases of Minoan, Greek,

---

[3] The same qualities appear in incipient (or superannuated) style phases of drawing or painting, except that two-dimensional art has an alternative which leads relatively easily up to a certain degree of successful representation: namely, putting everything into profile. Witness Magdalenian, Egyptian, Bushman painting, Eskimo engraving, etc. For frontality, stare, and stiffness in two dimensions, see the figure of Bellicia on page 6 of Flinders Petrie, *Revolutions of Civilization* (1911), and on page 438 of R. G. Collingwood in *Antiquity*, I (1927). I stand with Petrie: historically it is poor art. By 1927 the assault on all established and recognized forms of art was sufficiently under way for some critics to *prefer* low-grade productions of simplicity and helplessness; and in this case their rating was grist to Collingwood's mill of negativism.

and European sculpture.[4] He distinguishes archaism, classicism, and decadence as successive stages. On the whole his assemblage of evidence is very convincing. He makes a good case for pre-fifth-century Greek sculpture corresponding to that of the Christian pre-twelfth and twelfth centuries, Greek fifth to European thirteenth, Greek fourth to fourteenth, and Hellenistic art of the third century and following to European of the fifteenth and following. But beyond a certain point lacunae appear in the correspondence. There are no adequate Hellenistic counterparts to European seventeenth-century art, nor to nineteenth.

Incidentally, Deonna interweaves an idealism-realism polarity with his view of parallel stages of growth.

The famous Egyptologist W. M. Flinders Petrie is noted on the one hand for his successful intuitions and the dogmatism of his opinions, on the other for his skillful devising of "sequence dating," a system of construing the relative age of undated archaeological artifacts from a combination of stylistic features. He published in 1911 an astounding little book, *The Revolutions of Civilization*, which undertook to settle several problems of both civilization and style in about fifteen thousand words and some fifty illustrations. By the time he gets his scheme of findings set up, Petrie has calmly made some breath-taking assertions, omissions, and leaps. For instance he sets the beginnings of the culminations in our own Western civilization as follows: in sculpture, in the high Middle

[4] *L'Archeologie, Sa Valeur, Ses Methodes*, 3v. (1912). Vol. III, "Les Rhythmes Artistiques," is particularly to the point.

Ages, at A.D. 1240; in painting, at 1400; in literature, at 1600; music, 1790; science and wealth, not yet reached.[5] Petrie had behind him a lifetime in archaeology, both as an excavator and writer, which led him into constant dealing with styles as well as with long-range aspects of civilizations. It was as a result of this experience that he was the first to clearly formulate two ideas: one, that fine-art styles tend to be the most sensitive indicator of the profiles of civilizations and their stages; and two, that the final shedding of all archaic features means mastery of an art, is a point which can be concretely specified in its history, and thus is significant of the entry of the art into its great phase or culmination. I accept both these ideas.

Flinders Petrie was equally definite about the sequence in which the several arts and other activities develop within civilizations. He did not hesitate to project his Egyptian findings into a scheme that applied to all Mediterranean and European civilizations. The order is: sculpture, painting, literature, technology, wealth.[6]

[5] This is less aberrant and shocking than it first sounds, because his dates specify not the *apex* of the culmination but its *beginning* as marked by the dropping off of the last archaisms. But he is too Olympian to trouble whether he has made this clear to the reader, and the first impression is that he rates Gothic cathedral statues higher than Michelangelo, and Masaccio above Raphael.

[6] Petrie expresses himself positively on a variety of other topics, including cyclic periods and their duration, but I am considering him here only with reference to art. As for dates, many of his computations are completely out of kilter because before 2000 B.C. he used a "long" chronology which has now been abandoned by everyone.

There have been a good many findings of this sort, both as between the arts in one civilization and the sequence of genres within an art. Thus Ligeti says that the sequence is: tectonic; plastic; pictorial, which means architecture; sculpture; painting; and he has these flourish respectively in the immaturity, maturity, and decline of civilizations.

As Sorokin points out,[7] there may be reminiscences here of the Hegelian generic sequence of symbolic, classic, and romantic types of art, these finding their fullest realization respectively in architecture, in sculpture, and (among the visual arts) in painting.

Both Sorokin and I have applied to these propositions the empirical test of count of cases, without finding much confirmation.[8]

It must be borne in mind that a percentage priority of architecture is expectable, because there is some building, however humble, in every culture, so that when fine arts develop, architecture can get off with a running start.

Similarly, sculpture just is and remains an art of simpler and more direct problems than painting. It represents three-dimensional objects in three dimensions, painting has to compress them into two. Foreshortening, chiaroscuro, shadows, perspective, atmosphere are effects that essentially lie outside the domain of sculpture. Within a given style, sculpture thus tends to exhaust its simple roster of approaches more quickly.

Similar to painting, literature can go on developing for

[7] *Social Philosophies* (1950), pp. 17–19.
[8] *Ibid.*, p. 18; Kroeber, *Configurations* (1944), pp. 777–790.

a long time by devising new manners and genres, like the novel.

Finally, we must remember that some civilizations begin with a set for or against certain arts, or other activities, so that one of these may be delayed, another permanently inhibited, a third fostered into rapid development. For instance Islamic civilization began with a taboo against sculpture and representative painting, but started with a poetry already in full blossom.

All in all, there is an interesting field to be explored here, in which the history of events, of culture, and of art must all be given consideration. There may yet prove to be certain prevailing trends, but they must be authenticated by an established prevalence of separate occurrences, each analyzed for its context as well as in itself. If there are immanences, they will emerge at the end of study; they should not be assumed from casual inspection.

Such are some of the analytic approaches from art which also bear on civilizations. I now proceed to summarize my over-all conclusions.

## CONCLUSIONS

We know of styles and civilizations in some measure by personal experience with them, but more largely through what history has preserved and interpreted.

Both style and civilizations are sociocultural phenomena. That is, they are "social" in the usual indefinite sense of that word, which means essentially that they are more than individual. More strictly, styles and civilizations are cultural phenomena, because they are patterned products of human societies.

Like many anthropologists, I use the word civilization almost synonymously with the word culture. At any rate I try to put no weight on a distinction. There is a widespread usage of the term civilization as meaning advanced or literate or mainly urban culture. With this usage I do not quarrel; but I have tried to choose between the two near synonyms in such a way that the reader would realize in any given situation whether I meant the more general or the more slanted sense. The word civilization has also had a pejorative sense, as an essentially evil or anticreative phase of culture, especially so in German usage; and in dealing with Spengler it is sometimes awkward neither to misrepresent him nor to seem to endorse his view by using the word.

A style is a strand in a culture or civilization: a coherent, self-consistent way of expressing certain behavior or performing certain kinds of acts. It is also a selective way: there must be alternative choices, though actually they may never be elected. Where compulsion or physical or physiological necessity reign, there is no room for style.

The word style originated with reference to literature and still has its core of meaning in the domain of fine arts. It can be used both of individual idiosyncrasy and of a cultural way or manner. I have used it here throughout in the latter sense. There is no doubt that men of genius have a large hand in the production of most styles. But a man of genius is a member of his society and a contributor to his culture as well as an individual personality; and it is legitimate at times to abstract from the personality and treat him as a cultural phenomenon. It is even possible largely to define an artist of genius or talent, and the quality of his work, by his position in the flow or curve of the style to which he belongs.

While styles are most characteristic in the fine arts—thus, a product wholly lacking style would no longer be valid as a work of art—nevertheless elements of style enter other activities, such as eating and dressing, which also serve useful or nonaesthetic gratifications. Here the element of style, not being dominant, enters into adjustments and assumes aberrant forms. For instance, both the long-term gastronomic and the brief dress-fashion styles lack the characteristic course of development and culmination of fine art styles, the former rather seeking stable continuance, the latter constant change but without climax. Decorative styles in useful objects are in a somewhat similar situation. However, these mixed styles —mixed in the sense of being only partly determined by aesthetic factors—the mixed styles possess the advantage of being readily analyzed for verifiable study, even by measurement.

The historical behavior of movements in philosophy, scholarship, mathematics, and pure or fundamental science is quite similar to that of fine-art styles. I mean by this that the time profile curve of value of product, or rating of talent of the producers, is generically the same in the several activities. In other words, intellectual creativity and aesthetic creativity behave alike historically, presumably because they operate in equivalent ways: they both produce intrinsic values.

The course of applied science plots out differently in most history, no doubt on account of the affiliations with utility, profit, and technology.

In general, pure styles have a limited life, presumably because they exhaust their creative possibilities and have to begin over with an enlarged or otherwise new base.

Modern pure science, perhaps because of its success and massive organization, has considerably escaped this style limitation of earlier sciences, and tends to progress more uniformly and steadily. There are indications that a similar change is impending in the visual arts, and possibly in music; but is being delayed in literature by language diversities.

Since human culture cannot be wholly concerned with values, having also to adapt to social (interpersonal) relations and to reality (survival situations), the totality of a culture can scarcely be considered outright as a sort of expanded style. But its contained styles, impinging on the rest of the culture, can influence this; and all parts of a culture will tend to accommodate somewhat to one another; so that the whole may come to be pervaded with a common quality and to possess a fairly high degree of congruence. For want of a better term I have called this the whole-culture or total-culture style. It must be regarded as due to secondary spread and assimilation within the culture. It is not the primary determinant of the culture as Spengler saw it.

Culture or civilization as a concept may be distinguished from the history of the human species by two main criteria. First, culture is a set of patterns, abstractable from behavior. The historian ordinarily deals directly with behavior—human actions or events—and only incidentally or indirectly with its patterning. He may suspend the flow of narrative for a topical review or analysis in which he describes patterns; but this constitutes a minority element in historiography generally.

Another way of putting this difference is to follow Coulborn in saying that the student of culture focuses on the regularities and repetitions, the expectabilities, of human life in a given area and time, whereas the historian emphasizes its singular events and therefore irregularities.

The second main distinction between culture and history is that the student of culture can and does abstract when he wishes not only from events but from individuals, except as exemplifications, whereas the historian takes both individuals and masses as they come mixed in the record, and even does not exclude patterns. Not that historians are nondiscriminatory: they tacitly select individuals who have been influential, and narrate events that have had broad or enduring effects.

The historian may compare the events or institutions of different societies or periods, but this is permissive to him. The anthropologist or student of culture must sooner or later compare the cultures of societies separate in period or area, if his study is to have wider significance.

To make his comparisons fully significant, the student of culture must see his cultures in space, must classify them, and therefore delimit them so far as he can. The historian freely chooses an area or period, on the basis of the accidents of his knowledge or convenience or preference. When however he enters upon problems of periodization, he is *de facto* classifying, and is facing a problem like that of the delimitation of cultures.

The comparison of cultures or civilizations and the comparison of histories overlap, but both must be distinguished from philosophies of history. As the phrase was originally coined by Voltaire, the philosophy of history denoted a universal history in outline with certain slants of opinion: in his case, enlightenment and anticlericalism. Herder wrote another, of more exotic and sympathetic slant. A recent example is Wells's *Outline*.

Another sort of philosophy of history is Hegel's, in which the narration of events is curtailed in favor of exposition of a principle, which alone is followed through. Vico and Ibn Khaldun are other examples. None of the writers considered in the present study has done a philosophy of history, though Northrop's *The Meeting of East and West* shows some approach to the type; and Sorokin's work seems to, though his principle of supersystems can be reduced back to periodized and summarized sequential history of culture phases.

The separation or delimitation of civilizations from one another is, as just said, an organization of our knowledge comparable to periodization in history. The delimitation can rarely be made with sharpness, and is never absolute. Culture and the events of history are both continua, over the inhabited earth as well as in time. Every delimitation is therefore a choice, and decisions will vary somewhat in detail even though there be agreement as to the area within which they fall. Thus A.D. 330, 476, 622 have all been suggested as marking the end of ancient history, or of the Graeco-Roman culture, in Western Europe; and all have something to be said for them. Similarly as regards 1453, or 1492, or 1519 for the "boundary" between what we call mediaeval and modern history of Europe.

While historians mostly choose significant or expressive events for these demarcations, a valid historical period, which means one useful for understanding of events, is usually also significant of a cultural phase or natural stage in the development of a civilization.

When it is a matter of higher civilizations, these usually segregate themselves from one another by possessing focal points of cultural intensity or success. The foci, or climaxes, of compared civilizations are usually surrounded by areas and periods of less advanced culture, so that the cardinal classification is normally obvious. The intervening areas are then assignable one way or the other according as they show greater or less relationship to this or that focus.

The following factors all serve to distinguish civilizations from one another: language including the spread of languages of civilization or high culture, the form of religion, empire or political control, the degree of technological development or accumulation of wealth. Occasionally these criteria do delimit civilizations sharply.

The most sensitive though least objectifiable indicator on the whole is style, especially in the fine arts, but also, in a broad way, in decoration, dress, and food. The sensitivity of style as an index applies to time as well as to spatial distribution.

Where the areas occupied by separate civilizations are actually in contact, the delimitation sometimes makes difficulty on account of transitions. On the other hand, civilizations frequently simplify the situation by each imposing their different rule, religion, speech, or customs.

Where the area occupied by *successive* civilizations is partly or wholly the same, the decision to be rendered may lie between recognizing separate civilizations or separate phases of the same civilization. Factors that enter into such decisions are: permanent conquest; establishment of a new religion, as rightly emphasized by Toynbee; expansion or retraction of area covered; severity of political, economic, aesthetic-ideological breakdown between the two cultures.

In general, if a breakdown is severe and long enough that there remain less content and less patterning in the extant culture when new growth again takes place than there were when the breakdown began, the period of diminution and disintegration is of the type experienced in Western Europe in post-Roman times (500–900) and may, like it, be considered a "dark age" and be construed as separating two civilizations. Where the breakdown is rather of the reconstitutive sort, with new definite patterns arising to displace or crowd on old ones, and an over-all increase of population, wealth, technology, knowledge, horizon, or total-culture content is simultaneously taking place, as after the high mediaeval period in

Europe, the interval, like an insect's or bird's molt, is the preparation for a new and larger phase of a still growing civilization. Such a reconstitutive interval is however accompanied by some losses of patterning and especially style. In Europe, for instance, Gothic sculpture and architecture, scholastic philosophy, feudalism, and the influence of Christianity and the church declined in this interval. The total civilization may be said to have been reorganized on a broader base, allowing an ultimately wider range of patterns and styles.

The present condition of our own Western civilization since about 1900 seems to be more correctly construed as of this type, rather than as the beginning of our final breakup as Danilevsky, Spengler, Adams, and others predicted and Toynbee holds as a danger. Many long-established patterns of life have obviously disappeared irrevocably in the past half-century, and practically all art styles have been progressively shattered. But new patterns of both social structure and culture are emerging, and growth continues in population, wealth, leisure, technology, and science.

Where a society is conquered and remains subject for a considerable duration to a society with a different culture, as in Mesopotamia under the Kassites and in Iran under Hellenism, or where in a time of upset and division a religion is introduced and established—or perhaps lost —as Buddhism was in China and India, it may be difficult to decide whether it is more profitable to understanding to infer a new civilization or a new phase of the old one. Toynbee's concept of the intercivilizational chrysalis religion is a fertile one, but it must not be allowed unduly to override: there are always multiple factors.

Ancient Egypt with its four-time establishment of nearly identical over-all pattern presents of course a quite simple situation, but one not to be expected to recur very often. It will be noted that Egypt is geographically isolated, and that there were no changes of consequence in the extent of area occupied by the culture. Inasmuch as there was a persistent increase of content in the culture, partly by invention and even more by importation, the question may be raised whether Egyptian civilization came to an end through its old static forms being less and less able to hold their growing content, or by the simpler process of repeated conquest and imposition of foreign culture.

I agree with Sorokin that the Danilevsky and Spengler view, largely implied also by Toynbee—that a civilization necessarily has a single life course with but one unrenewable phase of creativity—is untenable.

A better understanding of civilizations seems obtainable from focusing study on the content, structure, and flow of their culture than on recurring patterns of events in their histories. This would be my largest criticism of Toynbee, because, while his study is of history, he professes to make the analysis through civilizations, and yet operates chiefly with a skeleton of the events affecting their societies: as he must as long as he insists on operating with an ultimately moral causality.

The study of civilizations must progress beyond preoccupation with a small number of highly contrastive great cultures and must include minor, derivative, and even humble cultures, of course with emphasis according to importance. Toynbee has led the way here, but procedure should aim at still greater inclusiveness and less haphazardness of selection.

The various proposed schemes of comparative interpretation of civilizations suffer less from being intuitively subjective—for in the face of such masses of macrophenomena a beginning can hardly be made otherwise—than from inadequacy of content and coverage. As more empirical data are brought into relevant bearing, they will increasingly correct imperfect intuitive views, especially as these are schematic.

Rhythmic periodicities, also lengths of durations, seem to me to have shown their relative unprofitableness as subjects of inquiry. On the contrary, near recurrences, partial and irregular uniformities, are expectable, having long been known to occur as "convergences," both in culture history and in organic history. More methodical analysis of these will be profitable. The topic of variation in the sequential order of different creativities is also in need of more systematic examination.

Assumption of immanent forces is best left as a last recourse. So far there has not been sufficiently vigorous prosecution of intensive study to warrant that recourse. More likely are secondary or pseudo immanences: internal cultural sets of varied strength which have been gradually developed as a result of external forces.

## Style and Civilizations

The study of civilizations can hardly become truly scientific or scholarly until it divests itself of emotional concern about crisis, decay, collapse, extinction, and doom.

# APPENDICES

# I

# Spengler's Magian-Arabic and Toynbee's Syriac Cultures

THE Apollinian-Faustian polarity between the Classical and the Western cultures is obviously largely based on Nietzsche's Apollinian-Dionysian contrast. It is perhaps significant that Nietzsche developed his thesis in a work on the birth of tragedy—in other words, on an art form. The fact suggests the affinity of Spengler's concept of culture to concepts of style.

The Magian-Arabic culture is a concoction by Spengler to serve as a *tertium quid* to the Classical and Western cultures. It is not recognized by historians, but, in its prodromal stage, is a synthesis of Persian and Seleucid and late Hellenistic strivings. Syrian and early Christian influences mark its origin around the time of Christ, and include Christian development as far at least as Augustine and the Monophysites. From Mohammed on, the culture becomes essentially subsumed under Islam. This seems a quite various assortment, heterogeneous in nationality, speech, religion, art, and government, insufficiently held together by its prime symbol of the vaulted cavern shielding the congregation of the elect.

Strangely enough, Toynbee, brought up as a historian, recognizes an equally implausible civilization, the Syriac, in the same geographic area. Like the Magian, this Syriac civilization includes the active span of Islam, and realizes its "universal state" in the Abbasid empire as a "reintegration" of the Achaemenian empire after a "suspension" of a thousand years; and Islam finally also becomes its "universal church." As with Spengler's Magian culture, both Persian and Syrian elements enter into the formation of the Syriac civilization; but Toynbee sets the birth of this earlier, in the tenth century B.C., though the terminations of both cultures are about the same, in our thirteenth century. Toynbee, however, includes post-Solomonic Judaism instead of primitive Christianity in his version of this Near Eastern construct.

What both the Magian and the Syriac civilizations lack, is general matter-of-fact recognition as phenomena. Until Spengler and Toynbee, no historian knew of them. Incredible as it may seem, they are new suits made out of an unwoven cloth. I can see only one reason for such fabrication: a highly special situation into which the Near East had got itself by around 1000 or 500 B.C., when its cultural primacy was first wavering and then passing away.

The Near East had been pre-eminent in the origination of fundamentals of culture—metal work, writing, cities, kingship, and the like, from the end of the Stone Age on. Spengler's two oldest cultures, Babylonian and Egyptian, grew here; and Toynbee recognizes five: Egyptiac, Sumeric, Minoan, Hittite, Babylonic. By B.C. 1000 some of these five cultures had perished, the energy of the rest had slackened, except for fitful flare-ups like that of late Assyria. By B.C. 500, they were all dead. Politically the Persian universal state briefly overlay the area. Then Hellenism both overran this state and submerged it culturally. What had for millennia been the fount and origin of higher civilization, was now subject to a new upstart culture. Such old Near Eastern ways and values and prides as still persisted lived on increasingly obscure, remote, hidden. Christianity, a product of the area arisen among the lowly, might have been a deliverer to the millions of culturally dispossessed Near Easterners, but it gained its greatest strength in the cities of the Helleno-Roman civilization and empire which constituted most the overlay, and then captured control of this civilization, thus riveting still further cultural subjection on Syrians, Egyptians, and other autochthons. The double level of culture continued, giving rise to the symptoms of "pseudomorphosis" that Spengler recognized correctly enough. Sects like Gnostics, Nestorians, Monophysites probably expressed popular resistance to orthodox Christianity and Empire. When finally the Helleno-Roman culture itself had aged and weakened sufficiently, Islam, with a sudden leadership developed by the "external proletariat" of the Arabs, represented a cultural overturn. This overturn, emanating from below and from beyond the margins, could best succeed by standing for a reduction, a simplification of culture, and did so succeed.

This is not exactly the way the story is usually told by historians, but it is fairly close to being a summary or synthesis of the several commonly accepted partial versions. At least it does not begin by fabricating the scaffold of a brand new historic entity; and it does perhaps help us to understand why Spengler and Toynbee felt the need of devising the Magian or Syriac civilization.

# II

# The Dearth of Spengler's Outer Cultures

IT IS not generally recognized how meagerly Spengler really deals with his cultures other than the Classic, Western, and Magian; how few cultural items or events he adduces in support of the whole-culture pattern he announces for each. His Indian, Chinese, Egyptian, and Babylonian physiognomies are remarkably thin and unsubstantial. He just does not cite enough data—and they were available in his day—ever to complete a coherent sketch, let alone a portrait. The following paragraphs are presented to substantiate my opinion that Spengler had acquired acquaintance with the patterns and styles of these remoter cultures only in intermittent flashes, and that he brought them into his total construct mainly as contrastive foils.

The specific characteristics which Spengler mentions for Indian culture are three: want of historical sense, invention of a sign for zero, and the concept of nirvana. All three are negations. This looks like the promising beginning of a large pattern of culture. But Spengler's follow-up of the pattern is muffed: it is vague and incomplete. The obvious parallel of maya, the basic Hindu belief in the illusoriness of the world, is not even drawn.

Another side or supplement of Indian "negating" is the tendency to rationalize, to consistency, system-mongering, and abstruseness—this last carried to the extreme of whittling sensory reality away. This pervading quality of rationalization and systematizing in Indian culture, Spengler seems not to have formulated. Yet it *is* systematizing rather than common sense to conceive absence of quantity as quantity and so denote it. It is fine-spun to conceive consonants as naturally "containing" a sequent vowel, and then to devise a symbol for absence of the vowel, the vikrama: thus, "k-" when the consonant is final in a phrase, as against simple "k" which is read "ka." From the angle of the life of senses and feelings, nirvana is its rarified limit of total detachment from all affects. This can be seen as a logical extreme of common sense as well as a mere negation of it. The invention of the most abstruse of games, chess—as it is also one of the simplest in its rules—again points to intellectual primacy in the culture. So does the invention of grammar. And, once more back to writing, the Sanskrit alphabet is a highly rational, accurate classification and ordering of phonemes, rebuilt out of the haphazard sequence that had reached the Hindus from its Semitic source —as it reached the Greeks and us, too, but without stirring

there any impulse at better systematization. And karma—
"often enough regarded quite materially, as a world-stuff
under transformation," says Spengler heterodoxically—
karma can much better be construed as moral causality, as
an abstract extension and rational correlate of the mechanical causality which our sense experience instills into us.
And even the very absence of Indian interest in the carnal,
fluctuating, purposeless incidents of history is perhaps most
easily understood as due to the contrary emphasis which
the Hindu put on the eternal immutable verities to which
he believed he could attain by the insight of understanding
and of purified reason alone.

In short, the Indian culture pattern is heavily characterized by the overtoning of systematizing rationality. Its
negations, like the inclination to exaggerate, while characteristic enough, seem rather to resolve into facets of this
larger pattern, which Spengler seems not to have recognized.

Spengler's characterization of the course of Indian culture is largely a product of free imagination. The culture
is seen as forming around 1500 B.C. and terminating by
the Christian era. "Its organic phase came to an end with
the rise of Buddhism"; it must have been "rich in great
events between the 12th and 8th centuries." [1] But these are
the centuries of which we actually know virtually nothing!

And here is Spengler's "deeper meaning" of Buddhism:
It is the "final and purely practical [!] world-sentiment

---

[1] *The Decline of the West*, trans. by Atkinson (1926), I, 11, 12.
This was subsequently reissued in one volume with the same paging
but with a combined index, which is fuller for vol. I than in the
original 1926 issue.

of tired megalopolitans who had a "closed-off Culture behind them and no future before them," [2]—a "closed-off" past for which facts are scant and not adduced by him, and ahead of them "no future"—which however contained Gupta sculpture, Ajanta painting, Kalidasa's poetry, the post-Gupta mathematicians, and Sankara's ninth-century Vedanta.

There is something real in Spengler's recognition of certain trends shared by the Indian and the Hellenic cultures. They were both nonhistorical-minded in larger perspective; both are given to analytical abstraction; both are imbued with a sense of form patterns and relations; both tend to a static world-concept—and this brings us back to their timelessness.

Spengler surely read oversignificance into the fact that the Indian and Hellenic cultures did not evolve a "script" of their own—he means an originally devised ideographic system or conglomeration—as had the Chinese, Mesopotamian, Egyptian, and Maya-Mexican cultures. Instead, he says, they took over, late in their own careers, the developed writing of a neighboring culture that was itself in an advanced state of senescence. They failed to beautify either their script or their books, he says again, because of their "steady hatred of that which endures, their contempt for a technique which insists on being more than a technique"; and they developed no art of monumental inscription. In fact, they resisted writing, and the alphabet "won their acceptance" slowly, "as a humble tool of everyday use." [3]

As against this explanation out of immanent nature, which cannot be proved or disproved, the essential facts of the situation are known. The alphabet is an invention presup-

[2] *Ibid.*, p. 356.    [3] *Ibid.*, II, 150–152.

posing both previous nonalphabetic writing and intercultural relations. It results in a product which, just because it is extricated from art, religion, and other irrelevances, is an effective technique—rapid, easy, prolific, democratic. Mesopotamia and Egypt had provided antecedent forms of prealphabetic writing. The Indian and Greek cultures happened to develop at a time and place where they could profit from adopting the new "Phoenician" alphabetic technique, and did so; as did most of the rest of the world.

Mesopotamian or "Babylonian" culture proves on analysis to have been treated with astonishing meagerness by Spengler. It is not accorded a column in his synoptic tables. Essentially contemporary with Egyptian, its phases would accordingly be, approximately: precultural, 3400–3000; the heart of the culture, 3000–1800; then formless, inorganic, cosmopolitan "civilization," 1800–1200. The subsequent Chaldaean or Neo-Babylonian period of southern Mesopotamia lies outside Spengler's Babylonian culture.[4] But literally all that Spengler says about the Babylonian is the following thin sheaf. The Greeks did not take over the developed Babylonian chronology and almanac-reckoning, nor the superior Babylonian geography; in fact Chaldaean [*sic*] astronomy was basically abhorrent to them; and while sundials were early in Babylonia, the word *hora* received its meaning of hour among the Greeks only in the fourth century.[5] Hammurabi's Babylon was an autumnal city of spiritually dead men;[6] with Thebes of the New Empire, it was the earliest of all world-cities.[7] This is what I have been able to note or have found with the help of the index.

The Egyptian and Chinese cultures fare somewhat more

[4] *Ibid.*, pp. 205, 206, 238.

[5] *Ibid.*, I, 9, 10, 15, 147.

[6] *Ibid.*, p. 79.

[7] *Ibid.*, II, 99.

fully. Yet a search makes it apparent that they never receive treatment in their own right for more than a few paragraphs at a time. Basically they are brought in, like India, as foils for the Classical-Occidental contrast, or the Classical-Occidental-Magian one. It is topics like anxiety as part of historical-mindedness, megalopolitan philosophy, perspective, and landscape gardening that are considered; considered first, almost always, as to the Apollinian or Faustian or Magian expression of them; then in the peripheral cultures, but contrastively instead of substantively. Here, in general, India is lined up with Greece-Rome, and Egypt and China with Europe, especially as regards time-attitude; only occasionally are physiognomies of their own sketched or hinted at.

# III

# Sorokin

PITIRIM A. SOROKIN, who in his youth was in danger of his life from the Tsarist government and later from the Communists but who has recently peacefully retired at Harvard, has written *Social and Cultural Dynamics* in four volumes, 1937–1941. In four chapters of a later work, *Society, Culture, and Personality*, 1947, he has conveniently summarized the lengthy findings of his *Dynamics* as regards civilizations.[1] In 1952, F. R. Cowell published a one-volume condensed restatement of Sorokin,[2] parallel to Somervell's 1947 *Abridgement* of Toynbee. Sorokin has also written

[1] Chs. xl–xliii.

[2] *History, Civilization, and Culture: An Introduction to the Historical and Social Philosophy of Pitirim A. Sorokin.*

a very fair-minded and useful book especially concerned with the theories and interpretations of history by Danilevsky, Spengler, Toynbee, Northrop, myself, and others, with critical evaluations of them.[3]

Sorokin tends to see things large. Hence he labels Spengler's *Decline*, Toynbee's *Study*, and my *Configurations* "social philosophies"—which they may be in some small degree though primarily they are interpretations of certain facets of history. He himself is given to basing his own work on a pretty broad and explicit general philosophy. The element of systematic reasoning and structuring is strong in him.

It is this bent that leads him to deny significant reality to civilizations. He uses cultural data freely: his *Dynamics* consists of several volumes of cultural facts, many of them elaborately or approximately measured, charted, and plotted. But he is not really interested in cultures in the plural number—in the several civilizations that have grown up in history. There is not much systematic philosophy in history: least of all in the opinion of historians.

I am in agreement here with the historians and not with Sorokin. I would not dream of claiming that the ideas I have been discussing represented a "system" of thought. They are gropings toward a somewhat more adequate understanding of certain properties of styles and civilizations as we know them in history. But I do believe absolutely in the reality and significance of the particular styles whose existence underlies my discussion. I also believe that Egyptian and Chinese and Hellenic civilization existed, though we may argue whether we obtain better understanding if we include Roman civilization within the Hel-

[3] *Social Philosophies in an Age of Crisis* (1950).

lenic or if we keep it separate and co-ordinate. Civilizations are not too easily characterized or delimited, because they constitute enormous masses of historic fact. But their reality is undeniable, and if history has any meaning, civilizations are certainly significant macrophenomena, even if their edges may often be fuzzy and their nature and behavior are not yet understood as well as we would like.

Sorokin has increasingly tended to deny integration or real unity to civilizations. He seems to think that Danilevsky, Spengler, and Toynbee—he could have included me also—assume that "the *total* culture of each . . . civilization is completely integrated and represents one meaningfully consistent and causally unified whole." [4] Spengler to be sure did assert complete consistency for each civilization, though he flatly denied them causal unity. But the others, and I, have never claimed complete integration, either of significance or through causality.

Contrariwise, Sorokin himself describes civilizations as "a sort of dumping ground where billions of diverse cultural phenomena are thrown together. . . . Only part of these is causally or causally-meaningfully united with other parts." [5] In his very latest book, of 1956, *Fads and Foibles*, he repeats that no civilization "is a unified cultural system, but is a vast cultural dump." It "cannot be born, or grow, or die, as one system." [6]

The key to this extreme statement seems to be in Sorokin's last three words: "as one system." If that means that a civilization cannot die as an animal dies, every one is in agreement, because a civilization is not an animal: it is an infinitely larger and more complex macrophenomenon. But

[4] *Ibid.*, p. 209.          [5] *Ibid.*, pp. 209–210.
[6] Page 164.

when Sorokin says that a civilization has no unity at all,[7] it is he that is taking an all-or-none position, as much so as Spengler though on the opposite side; and he is far more intransigent than Toynbee, or than Danilevsky was.

The effect of Sorokin's position, in any event, is to minimize the importance of civilizations as historic phenomena, and thereby to maximize the significance of systematic constructs, which, not being historical, or factually given, can lay claim to universality and significance.

Sorokin's constructs are twofold: first, what in everyday language would be parts or segments of a civilization; and second, something bigger than a civilization, transcending it. The first he calls systems and congeries; the second, supersystems.

Systems differ from congeries in that the first are meaningfully integrated; the latter have their elements associated fortuitously. The principal pure systems in culture are Language, Science, Fine Arts, Religion, and Ethics. Being integrated, each of these has a "self-directing unity"—something immanent—with a "margin of autonomy" against forces outside. Language is the most autonomous. Besides these pure systems there are also mixed or derivative ones. Thus Philosophy is a blend of Science, Religion, and Ethics. Economics and Politics are other derivative systems.

There is of course no novelty in recognizing these divisions or parts or segments of culture—which in fact every-

[7] The exact words are: "the basic error of taking for a civilizational-cultural system something that is no unity at all" (*Social Philosophies*, p. 216). None of the writers in question probably ever thought of conceiving of a culture or civilization as a *system*. That is an addendum by Sorokin, due to his personal bent of mind.

body has always taken for granted: except that it is original with Sorokin that he attributes to these parts the integration and autonomy which he denies to the total civilization. I am unclear why he does this. If I may take refuge in a simile, it seems to me much as if one were to assert that the nervous system has more integration and meaning than the whole organism, in which the nervous is co-ordinated with the vascular, gastrointestinal, sensory-receptor, and other systems. This may be true logically, because a small part can always be more closely knit than a larger whole consisting of several such parts. But what of mere logic? The given, functioning, and natural unit remains the living animal, without which the parts could not and do not exist in nature. Similarly, whole cultures, be they little primitive ones or great civilizations, certainly exist and have a history; but languages, philosophies, economies, and so on, though they occur universally in all cultures, occur only *in* them, and never occur independently in the world, any more than nervous systems float free and detached.

The supersystems, which transcend civilizations, seem to Sorokin to be the few basic forms which any civilizations can take. For my part I would describe them as pervasive or over-all qualities or facies, one of which every civilization must be showing at any given moment, according to Sorokin, and between which qualities the civilizations pulsate in a long rhythm. These quality-sets Sorokin derives empirically from a prolonged and detailed examination of civilizations through time. Much of the predominance at any one time of one or the other pervasive quality ("supersystem") he has justified by expressing it quantitatively, in tables and charts. Like the culture segments, he ascribes to the supersystemic qualities a coherence and significance which he denies to whole cultures or civilizations.

The two basic and longer-lasting of these supersystems are the Ideational and the Sensate forms or qualities of civilization. There is also a third, the Idealistic, which is a synthesis of the two main ones, briefer than they, and always following the Ideational in time and preceding the Sensate. As a matter of fact there is also a brief span in reverse position, following the Sensate and leading to the Ideational, which Sorokin sometimes calls Eclectic and sometimes calls Incoherent Reaction against Sensateness, and which he insists lacks the integration and meaningfulness of the three other phases.

Sorokin's characterizations of his two principal supersystems are vivid.[8] The Ideational supersystem has as its chief concern the supersensory: the kingdom of God. Its approach is symbolic; also ascetic, archaic, and simple. Ideational art is anonymous and collective. It contains no landscape, no genre, no realistic portraits, no satire or caricature. It is religious, attached to churches and cathedrals or their equivalents.

The Sensate supersystem deals in art with the empirical world of sense—often representing common people, even rogues. It is sensual, sexual, exciting, filled with passion. It is illusionistic, nonsymbolic, secular, and realistic. It tends to the pathological, morbid, and exotic. The doctrine of art for art's sake comes up in Sensate periods, and of art for pleasure. Changeable fashions and fads sweep along. Quantity prevails over quality, the colossal is at a premium.

[8] See especially *Society, Culture, and Personality*, ch. xl, and *Social Philosophies*, p. 46.

Or, as we pass from the realm of art, philosophy, and religion to the wider total range of the Sensate supersystems, Sorokin sees European civilization, from the sixteenth century on, as typically capitalistic, Protestant, democratic, individualistic, contractual in its relations, utilitarian in ethics, and sensate in its science and philosophy as well as art.[9]

By now it will have become apparent that the dichotomy of Ideational and Sensate bears resemblance to other polarities. One of these is the familiar rural-urban contrast. Many of Sorokin's Ideational traits are rural, most of his Sensate traits are typically urban. Another polarity is Redfield's of folk and provincial and peasant culture as against the sophisticate culture of the great traditions. The Sensate supersystem also approximates that final stage of each of his cultures which Spengler designates as the phase of "civilization," and which he sees as characterized by the secular, quantitative, mechanical, colossal, unfelt, megalopolitan, and democratic, and as subject to fashion.

It will also be evident that Sorokin's Ideational largely represents the sincere, strait, groping, unsure, unformed early phase of arts or civilizations, and that the period of his brief Idealistic transition refers to the fullest but transient realization of the art or culture, its culmination. His Sensate phase covers the maturity of success, of momentum continuing into senescence, still with accumulation and expansion at first, then with lessening of drive and quality, atrophy, and stereotyping. Finally, the incoherent "Eclecticism" which Sorokin keeps mentioning but saying least about, is not really so much a part of the course of a style or civilization as it is the interregnum of disintegration

[9] *Society, Culture, and Personality*, p. 590.

after a style or culture has run its course but its successor has not yet succeeded in achieving a defined direction of growth. He himself points out that this Eclectic is not meaningfully integrated as his other supersystems are.

Let me follow out Sorokin's concrete exemplification of his Ideational-Sensate pendulum beat and show how it converts into the more usual terms of those who recognize civilizations and their phases. The geographical route is: Greece, Rome, Western Europe—the phenomena are primarily from art.

About 800 B.C., Sorokin: Greek culture turns Ideational.—In the terms of others: beginning of Greek archaic style, stiff, so-called Geometric.

500 B.C., or just before, Sorokin: Ideational plus growing Sensate tendencies result in Idealistic synthesis.—Usual terms: beginning of the great culmination of Greek art—also of philosophy and other culture.

350 B.C., Sorokin: Sensate strain definitely predominant, lasts for seven centuries.—Usual phrasing: Hellenistic and Roman phase of Classical or larger Hellenic civilization.

A.D. 350. Sorokin: beginning of incoherent reaction against Sensateness.—In other terms: breakdown of civilization in West, Christianity dominant, Dark Ages.

A.D. 550. Sorokin: Ideational phase, lasting six centuries.—Usual phrasing: Carolingian and early Middle Ages.

A.D. 1175. Sorokin: new Idealistic synthesis, for less than two centuries.—Corresponds to High Mediaeval period, with Gothic architecture and sculpture, Scholastic philosophy, first vernacular literatures.

A.D. 1350. Sorokin: Sensate predominance for over five centuries.—Usual terms: Late Mediaeval, Renaissance, Modern.

A.D. 1900, approximately. Sorokin: first signs of a new anti-

Sensate reaction.—Others see an age of strain and crisis; Danilevsky, the beginning of a new civilization, the Slavic; Spengler, the winter of ossified civilization; I see rather the probable reconstitution of our Western civilization into a third phase, on a broader basis as regards both content and geography, and with many new patterns. This I believe on the ground that patterns are changing but general growth remains unchecked.

It will be seen how consistently the Ideational-Sensate scheme converts into the more usual one of life history of civilizations, and even corresponds fairly accurately with the periodization of orthodox historians.

In fact, this correspondence can be used to make one correction in Sorokin's outline. He actually begins his interpretation not with B.C. 800 but with B.C. 1200. The four centuries involved he calls Sensate—the aftermath of Mycenaean art and culture. True enough; but Mycenaean is itself an aftermath of Minoan, which everyone using Sorokin's terminology would surely label as having been a Sensate culture. Minoan had culminated in Crete, where it received its death blow with the destruction of Cnossus around 1400. By B.C. 1200, Minoan-Mycenaean had ended, and the four centuries that followed are described by historians as an interregnum, a breakdown, from which the new Hellenic culture began to emerge around B.C. 800. This would make the B.C. 1200–800 period one of Sorokin's unintegrated, incoherent Reactions against Sensateness, rather than actively Sensate. But as "incoherent" equals interregnum, the period is the "Dark Age" separating Minoan from Hellenic civilization: which indeed is how historians characterize the period.

In his last book on the subject, Sorokin himself sets forth

the similarity between his supersystems on the one hand and civilizations and their phases on the other.[10]

So we are all in accord in substance after all. Essentially, it is only the terminology of Sorokin that is aberrant. The rest of us have been historians, historians of art, natural historians like Danilevsky, historical anthropologists like myself. We all traveled the route of history, and expected our findings to be made in terms of history. Sorokin, as the one systematizing sociologist in the lot, felt impelled to come up with a nonhistorical, universalistic formulation: hence his Ideational-Sensate polarity or pulsation. Both sides admit the correspondence of this to civilizations and their phases.

This still leaves open the point of how far civilizations are integrated. Only Spengler has asserted absolute and complete integration. I suspect if he could come back and sit down with us in an atmosphere of interest in what he was concerned about, he would abate something of his intransigeance. I am sure that on a matured consideration Sorokin would not wish to seem to embrace the opposite intransigeance of total denial of integration in civilizations. In fact he has not voiced the denial consistently, but somewhat sporadically, in arguing against seeing too much integration in civilizations. It is to the units respectively one step smaller and one step larger than civilizations, to his systems and supersystems, that he would transfer integration. I agree with him unreservedly that no civilization can be completely integrated.

[10] *Social Philosophies*, pp. 293–297.

# The Messenger Lectures

IN ITS original form this book consisted of six lectures delivered at Cornell University in October, 1956, namely, the Messenger Lectures on the Evolution of Civilization. That series was founded and its title prescribed by Hiram J. Messenger, B.Litt., Ph.D., of Hartford, Connecticut, who directed in his will that a portion of his estate be given to Cornell University and used to provide annually a "course or courses of lectures on the evolution of civilization, for the special purpose of raising the moral standard of our political, business, and social life." The lectureship was established in 1923.

# Index

# Index

# Index

# Index